Staff Development:
A Handbook of
Effective Practices

Edited by
Sarah DeJarnette Caldwell

WITHDRAWN

1989

National Staff Development Council
P.O. Box 240
Oxford, Ohio 45056
(513) 523-6029

89-2313

TABLE OF CONTENTS

Section One
CONTEXT

Chapter

Section Two
PROCESS

ACKNOWLEDGEMENTS

Although the recent impetus for publishing this handbook came from the National Staff Development Council's 1986 long-range, strategic plan, the book has its "roots" in the early days of NSDC when the organization struggled for its identity and survival. The organization's statements of philosophy, position papers, journals, and newsletter helped shape a new group of professionals specializing in staff development.

In the late 70s and into the 80s the "Effective Staff Development Practices" workshops provided much needed assistance and information for NDC members, especially for those new to the a staff development role. In addition, as the knowledge base of effective practice has increased in almost geometric proportions, the need for a handbook to supplement training materials has been recognized. Thus the "Effective Practices" workshops have been a major source for the content and structure of this book.

In recognition of this need for a handbook the Board of Trustees of NSDC established a task force to review the organization's beliefs, assumptions, and knowledge about effective staff development practices, and further, to develop the book's content outline. Rather than deal exclusively with one particular approach to staff development such as peer coaching or with one client group such as teachers or administrators, the task force chose to provide a broad overview of effective practice ranging from contextual considerations to the "nuts and bolts" of designing and evaluating inservice activities.

Once a topical outline was agreed upon, NSDC members known for their expertise in these topics were invited to contribute chapters. Drafts of chapters were circulated among authors, task force members, and Trustees for review and critique.

In the true spirit of NSDC, the development of the handbook was a learning experience for all involved, including the editor. As a first-time editor I am grateful for the patience of chapter authors and reviewers during the many months that this book was being developed. One challenge was to remain faithful to the content requirements determined by NSDC beliefs and the organization's standards of effective practices of those practices. We believe this book has accomplished was initially what envisioned.

Many thanks to the Effective Practices Task Force and the Board of Trustees members who structured content and reacted to manuscript drafts: Phil Allopenna, Jean Cameron, Jean Hall, Jim Hildebrand, June Hogue, Jeanne Huddle, Jim LaPlant, Bob Meadows, Carlene Murphy, Dayna Richardson, Pat Roy, Tom Swenson, Charlotte Thiemecke, Paula Tissot, Guy Todnem, Don Unger, Sheila Wilson, and Sybil Yastrow. A special acknowledgment is due to former NSDC President Susan Ellis for substantial input and assistance.

We are also indebted to Pat Pingel and Pennie Smith who assisted in word processing and production and to Leigh Shallenberger for technical editing.

Dennis Sparks provided much needed encouragement for this handbook and continues to model the effective practices of NSDC through his leadership and support for all of us in the organization.

Foreword

Staff Development is now receiving more attention than any other speciality in education. The National Staff Development Council has become the organization to speak for staff developers and to speak to staff developers. It is therefore appropriate for NSDC to sponsor and publish *Staff Development: A Handbook of Effective Practices*.

This volume addresses five major topics: the context in which staff development occurs, the processes of effective staff development, the content addressed in staff development efforts, the foundations of our specialty, and the competencies needed by staff developers. For too long these concerns have been ignored or taken for granted. We can no longer afford to ignore them, take them for granted or leave them to be addressed by other organizations or individuals who are outside our area of specialization.

As staff development continues to gain recognition as a specialty within education it must be professionalized. That means, among other things, that there is a greater need for attention to those characteristics common to professions. These characteristics, which are incorporated into the content of this handbook, include:

* Practices based upon the results of research;
* Personnel with appropriate knowledge, skills and attitudes;
* Ethics accepted and enforced by practitioners;
* Techniques for evaluating staff development programs; and,
* Partnerships or collaboration with other educational personnel such as curriculum specialists, teachers, administrators, counselors, and other professional staff and with human resource development personnel in the private sector.

The intent of this publication as well as the intent of the National Staff Development Council is to focus upon the professional development of educators. We are indebted to Sally Caldwell and to the other writers who have shared their ideas and practices that have been found to be effective in staff development programs.

Carlene U. Murphy
President, 1988
National Staff Development Council

Introduction

Sarah DeJarnette Caldwell

Within this decade's context of school improvement, one thing is abundantly clear: Staff development has become the vehicle for meaningful change. It has brought attention to the "how" as well as the "what" of school improvement. And it has put into place the processes that support and nurture the climate and conditions necessary for both individual and organizational growth. A great deal has been learned about staff development practices and programs that make a difference in how teachers teach and how principals and central office personnel support and supervise school programs. This book is about those practices and programs.

Assumptions

Some basic assumptions serve as a framework for viewing the best of what is known about effective practices and programs. These assumptions help clarify and organize an emerging body of staff development research and knowledge that help us answer several key questions: What is staff development? Who is it for? How does it happen productively? These assumptions evolved from mission and beliefs statements of the National Staff Development Council(NSDC). They represent the philosophical foundation for the standards and practices in this handbook.

* **Staff development involves and benefits everyone who influences students' learning**. Whether directly or indirectly involved in students' learning, we all gain from continually developing our own skills and knowledge. When school personnel refine and improve their skill and knowledge, students benefit.
* **Both individuals and organizations have the inherent responsibility to define and achieve their own excellence**. Two words here are crucial: responsibility and excellence. The belief that the responsibility rests with the individual and the group has strong implications for how staff development is planned, conducted, and evaluated. Using excellence as the bottom line for individuals and groups makes a strong statement: mediocrity is unacceptable.
* **School improvement results from staff development.** We are not talking about improving schools with bricks, mortar and bulletin boards. The kind of school improvement that effects changes in student outcomes — achievement, attitude, and skill — comes about by affecting change in the personnel of a school. When we consider that 85% of most schools budgets are in personnel costs, developing the people of the system seems a wise protection of that investment. NSDC believes school

improvement results directly and primarily from personal and professional growth; individuals, working collectively and collaboratively, can make substantive changes in the school.

* **Effective staff development is based in research and theory and proved in practice**. A growing body of research in teaching, learning, adult learning and organizational development has key implications for staff development planners. Not to translate what we know from research into effective practice could be termed staff development "malpractice." For example, we know that substantive improvement in instruction and supervision occurs through long-term, continuous learning activity involving training and ample practice with feedback; therefore, we must plan our staff development activities accordingly. This is in contrast to planning a "one-shot," large-group lecture and hoping for a miracle.

* **The value of staff development should be measured by its impact on staff and the students they serve**. We want results from our efforts, results in terms of impact. We want something to be different as a result of staff development and we want measurable results. This is an appropriate goal when we consider the heavy investment of people and resources in a substantive, effective staff development program.

An Overview of the Handbook

This handbook's content could be organized in many ways. The model used is from Sparks (1983), in which staff development concepts are "nested" and organized in three components: context, process, and content (see Figure 1).

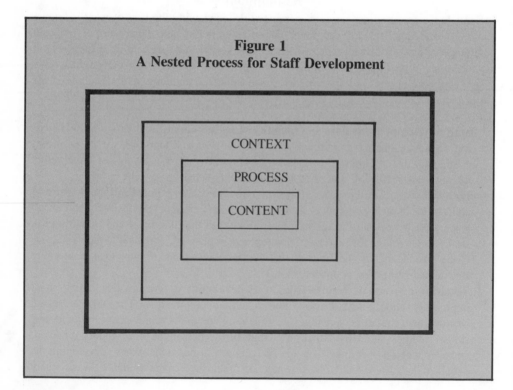

Figure 1
A Nested Process for Staff Development

CONTEXT

PROCESS

CONTENT

Context is the environment in which staff development takes place. Context concerns the "where" and "why" of staff development. The where refers to the locus of control, the location, or the focus of activity; e.g. department, school, or district-wide. The why refers to motivation for the activity — reasons or purposes which are derived from the school or organizational goals or initiatives.

Nested within this context is the process or the "how" of staff development. Programs for growth of the organization or the individual are planned, delivered, and evaluated using a variety of strategies and designs.

Nested within process and context is the content, or the "what" of staff development. The content may range from classroom-related topics such as teaching writing or handling discipline to organizational concerns such as supervising instruction or implementing curricular reforms.

Context

In the first part of this handbook (Chapters 1 through 4), context is discussed in terms of the organizational environment that provides purpose for and supports the delivery of staff development programs. Many contextual factors make an important contribution to effective staff development programs. For example, an organization's policies and resource allocations demonstrate commitment to long-term growth and renewal. District level expectations for accomplishment and collaborative planning contribute to context.

The organizational environment also provides the purpose, the why of staff development. Usually the mission of a district or a school sets the stage for programs. Individual goals and/or needs are also considered.

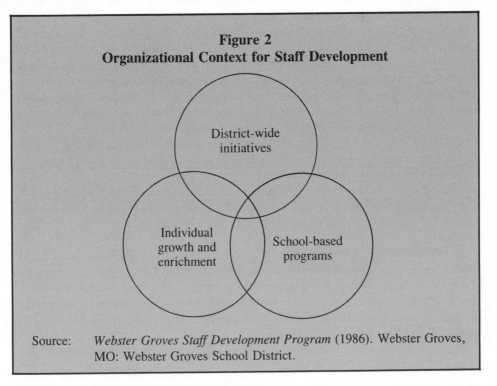

Figure 2
Organizational Context for Staff Development

District-wide initiatives

Individual growth and enrichment

School-based programs

Source: *Webster Groves Staff Development Program* (1986). Webster Groves, MO: Webster Groves School District.

A comprehensive program meets the needs at all three levels as indicated in Figure 2. There is a degree of overlap among the three levels, which could be expected within an organization with many common needs and concerns.

Metzdorf, in Chapter 1, deals with staff development from a district perspective. District-wide initiatives require system-wide coordination for awareness of innovation practices, revision of curriculum, implementation, and response to state mandates. All are topics of district-level staff development. Most district programs serve as an umbrella for the district human resource needs.

In Chapter 2, Wood describes staff development as the means for school-based improvement. The context for meaningful school improvement is the individual school where faculty members systematically plan, implement, and evaluate inservice programs that respond to school-basd immprovement goals.

Krupp discusses in Chapter 3 the responsibility of staff development to respond to the unique needs of individuals within an organization. Adults have both personal and professional needs to be addressed, and their approaches to learning vary based on their unique experiences.

Ellis, in Chapter 4, integrates these perspectives of district, school, and individual. A comprehensive district program provides the means through which philosophy, goals, resources, planning and staffing needs are coordinated.

Process

Part Two contains chapters dealing with process, or the "how," of staff development. How is effective training designed? How is new learning sustained and enthusiasm for an innovation kept alive? How can continuous improvement become the norm? How are programs evaluated? How can the change process be managed?

In chapter 5, Levine and Broude discuss designs for learning activities. The intended outcomes of staff development influence decisions about program design. For example, presentation techniques are appropriate where the goal is to have participants understand information, but changing behavior requires more complex and extensive strategies.

In Chapter 6, Kent, Austin, and Koffmann address the critical question, "How do you keep it going?" After the initial learning sequence is over, what's next? The support for continuous improvement and refinement of new learning takes many forms.

Next, in Chapter 7, Marshall presents four evaluation models that are particularly suited for staff development programs. As with designs for learning, evaluation strategies depend on the intended outcomes of the program.

Loucks-Horsley reviews in Chapter 8 the basic ingredients for successful implementation of an innovation. For the staff developer, the challenge is to help teachers and administrators become successful managers, not victims, of change.

Content

The content of any professional growth activity should be based on research and validated in practice. There is abundant research-based content dealing with the application of proven classroom strategies and supervisory practices, but it is not the purpose of this handbook to give thorough coverage to the many effective inservice programs that use the findings of research. Instead, we emphasize the practical use of research-based content and research methodology.

In chapter 9, Sparks and Simmons cite some of these research-based programs and discuss the use of the findings of research as the content base for training programs. They also make a strong case for the use of classroom research as a staff development technique.

Foundations of Staff Development

The body of knowledge concerning staff development practice has its foundation in the research on effective teaching, effective schools, organizational development, adult learning, and change. Bertani and Tafel, in Chapter 10, have reviewed the research findings and the literature on effective practices. They have integrated these studies around the structure of the handbook: context, process, content.

Competencies of Staff Developers

The recipient of the NSDC Lynne Chidley Foundation award, Dian Castle, presents the results and conclusions of her research on competencies of staff developers in Chapter 11.

Special Features of the Handbook

This handbook is a practical, concise overview of effective staff development practices. Because it is not an exhaustive treatment of the subject, most chapters contain an annotated bibliography for readers who want to study a strategy or concept more completely.

Each chapter includes a list of the knowledge, skills, and attitutdes staff developers need to implement successful programs. Using the competency lists, readers may assess their own experience and skill in specific areas.

Also, the chapter authors have analyzed their content to determine what practices would be used in a staff development program that successfully incorporates the ideas described in their chapter. Using the ''assessing your program'' questions, readers may measure the degree to which their staff development programs address or implement these key practices.

References

Sparks, G.M. (1983, November). Synthesis of Research on Staff Development for Effective Teaching. *Educational Leadership, 41*(3), 65-72.

Webster Groves Staff Development Program. (1986). Webster Groves, MO: Webster Groves School District.

Chapter 1

District-Level Staff Development

Neither individual entrepreneurial efforts nor school-based improvement projects are likely to have lasting impact unless they are embedded within a supportive district-level program.

Jim Metzdorf

Successful staff development programs are organized to provide for improvement on three different levels: individual, school, and district. As Krupp demonstrates in Chapter 3, it is individuals who change and who need appropriate support and incentives for engaging in that change. And as Wood describes in Chapter 2, the school is often the most appropriate organizational unit to engage individuals in effective, productive change. But neither individual entrepreneurial efforts or school-based improvement projects are likely to have lasting impact unless they are embedded within a supportive district-level program.

The need for comprehensive district-level staff development has been expanded in many states by new legislative initiatives. Local districts may now be responsible for assisting in teacher certification or recertification, providing career ladders, evaluating teachers and administrators according to state criteria, selecting mentors and cooperating teachers for state training, and other reforms. Most importantly, many states now mandate some kind of local staff development.

Purposes of a District-Level Staff Development Program

A district-level staff development program performs several essential functions:
* Development of the district's philosophy, goals, and expectations.
* Administration/coordination of staff development programs and resources within the district.
* Coordination/linkage with outside programs and resources.
* Provision of quality control and evaluation of staff development.
* Provision of district-level training, and curriculum implementation.
* Budgetary support.
* "Cheerleading" (providing vision and support).

Development of the District's Philosophy, Goals, and Expectations

The district philosophy creates the context for all staff development in a district. Shared beliefs supported by group members guide planning and day-to-day decisions (Combs & Avila, 1985). Figure 1.1 shows examples of belief statements from District #214, Arlington Heights, IL, District R-1, Jefferson County, CO, and the National Staff Development Council.

Although processes used to develop belief statements vary, staff involvement is essential to produce statements that have general acceptance and to ensure that staff development is seen as everyone's responsibility.

District-level goals are appropriate for all efforts that cut across schools. (See Ellis Chapter 4 for a description of a district-level goal-setting process.) For example, district-level goals would be appropriate for providing for successful racial integration, improving instruction through clinical teaching and mastery learning, integrating special education students into regular classes, or reorganizing junior high schools into middle schools. They can also address K-12 curriculum concerns, such as critical thinking in the social studies, as well as interdisciplinary efforts, such as writing across the curriculum.

District-level expectations come not just from district goals and policy but also from spoken and written statements and from behavior of district administrators. Effective central office administrators model the kind of ongoing problem-solving and professional improvement they expect from principals and teachers. They also engage principals and other administrators they supervise in a dialogue about those individuals' professional growth as well as their leadership roles in their schools or departments.

Administration/Coordination of Staff Development Programs Within the District

The district staff developer monitors needs at the individual, department, school, and district levels and is responsible to the board of education and the superintendent for developing and implementing staff development policies and goals based on those needs.

Most staff developers are assisted in this effort by committees comprised of representatives from across the district.

Whether an improvement effort is districtwide or is focused on a few schools or on just a few grades within schools, district-level coordination can ensure an appropriate distribution of resources and help eliminate waste or redundant efforts. These district-level functions include providing and brokering services — financial, material, and human. The district-level staff developer serves as a "linker," bringing together individuals or groups within the district who are working on common or similar problems.

Coordination/Linkage with Outside
Programs and Resources

The district staff developer links the district with a variety of organizations and resources outside the district. This function includes managing partnerships with business and industry; serving as liaison to colleges and universities regarding activities such as

---

Figure 1.1
Examples of Belief Statements for Staff Development

* It is the responsibility of all staff members to engage in professional development activities which will enhance their effectiveness in their respective positions.
* Staff development is most effective in bringing about change when programs are ongoing and there is ample opportunity for follow-up.
* Effective staff development programs recognize principles of adult learning and the continuous professional competence and commitment of all staff members.
* Staff development programs are most effective when they help staff integrate new learning with previously successful practices.
* People acquire and retain new skills and knowledge through a growth process more effectively than through a process which emphasizes correction.
* Change is a process — not an event. Implementation of educational programs takes from 2 to 5 years cycles of the innovation.
* Needs identified by various constituent groups and individuals are the basis for designing staff development activities.
* Commitment to implement planned change is built through collaboration and open communication.
* Teachers possess clinical expertise which, when shared, improves teacher effectiveness.
* Efficient and effective investment in developing the district's human resources yields dividends in accomplishing district goals.
* An effective staff development program supports individual personal self improvement within the context of organizational goal setting and growth-oriented appraisal.
* An effective staff development program attends to the human needs of those for whom it is designed, modeling positive human relations skills.
* An effective staff development program builds on the preservice training of teachers as the beginning of a continuum of development.

off-campus courses, student teacher placements, and internship programs; and serving as liaison to regional service agencies, regional consortia, and the state department of education. The staff developer may work to influence state rules and regulations and translates state regulations into district policies and practices.

The staff developer also brings outside resources — financial, material, and human — to appropriate groups within the district. This duty includes writing grant proposals, locating consultants, identifying worthwhile conferences, finding school districts with model programs that can be visited, and advising staff members on graduate and summer programs. Particularly useful sources of information and support for many staff developers are the nine federally funded regional laboratories for educational improvement. These labs serve every state, commonwealth, and trust territory and operate largely through established regional and local education agencies. The labs' primary purpose is to identify and disseminate good educational research and practice. They produce a variety of publications, offer consulting services, and sponsor local and regional conferences to accomplish that purpose.

The district staff developer monitors needs at the individual, department, school, and district levels and is responsible for developing and implementing staff development policies and goals based on those needs.

To be most effective in the linking role, a staff developer must network with other staff developers regionally and nationwide. Professional organizations such as the Association for Supervision and Curriculum Development and the American Educational Research Association have special interest groups that focus on staff development. The National Staff Development Council provides networking for staff developers through its publications and annual conference. Some of the federal labs have regional assistance centers to provide networking services. The Teachers' Center Network still provides a newsletter at a small cost to subscribers (who do not have to be involved with a teachers' center). Many states have developed computerized resource banks that list local speakers and consultants, topics, and references.

Provision of Quality Control and Evaluation of Staff Development

With authority comes accountability. Boards of education delegate to staff developers authority for developing the district's human resources. Summative and formative evaluation are major responsibilities stemming from this authority. (See Chapter 7 for approaches to evaluation.)

One example of evaluation that is appropriate on the district level and which contributes to quality control is front-end approval of course content and requiring careful selection and stringent training of instructors. Although courses may be only a small part of a comprehensive staff development program, they draw attention through their visibility and their frequent relationship to salary levels. Making sure that district-sponsored courses are of high quality contributes to setting a high level of expectation for all staff development activities in a district.

Another aspect of this function is the assessment or auditing of the staff development program from the overall perspective. The questions listed in the "Assessing Your Program" list (see Figure 1.2) can form the basis of such a process.

Provision of District-Level Training and Curriculum Implementation

District-level training is appropriate when there are too few participants to warrant programs at individual schools, when learning is enhanced by involving a cross section of district staff, when it costs less than programs at individual schools without sacrificing effectiveness, when content is not assignment specific, or when content must be delivered to all staff members. District-level training is particularly appropriate when it is designed to improve the skills of building administrators, not only because there are usually too few of them in any one school to justify an on-site program, but also because school-based administrators often work in isolation from others in similar roles and therefore enjoy and benefit from interacting with colleagues from across the district.

Curriculum implementation is often more cost effective at a district level and usually benefits from participation of individuals from a variety of schools.

Similarly, curriculum implementation, which includes the design of training needed to enable staff to implement the new or revised curriculum, is often more cost effective at a district level and usually benefits from participation of individuals from a variety of schools. Investment in the success of the new program is enhanced if teachers from all affected schools participate in the curriculum revision.

Another district-level program that may appropriately fall under the aegis of staff development is the induction of new teachers and the training of their mentors. If the state provides mentor training, the district may decide to enhance that training to enable mentors to guide new teachers in the implementation of specific district curricula. Similarly, the district staff developer is often responsible for training teachers whose grade level or subject assignment has changed.

Budgetary Support

Wherever responsibility for staff development lies, there also should exist appropriate funding. District-sponsored change efforts must be supported by a district-level budget for staff development. This budget may also include provisions for individual activities and for

Figure 1.2
Assessing Your Program

1. Is there a balance between programs and courses that respond to individual staff needs and the system directions created by districtwide program implementation, board policy, and state law?
2. Is there an appropriate variety of delivery patterns to accommodate different schedules and individual versus group development needs (i.e., weekly classes, intensive workshops, retreats, building-based staff development, content-based staff development, organizational development, or one-on-one coaching)?
3. Do the budget making process and resource allocation processes involve a wide variety of decision makers so as to gain broad-based support for staff development activities?
4. Are selected district staff members given training as staff development leaders and trainers and then actively used in the staff development program?
5. Are outside consultants used in an appropriate manner to bring in new ideas, manage special projects, or provide training of district leaders?
6. Are staff development programs designed to meet the needs of the wide variety of client groups in the school district including teachers, administrators, counselors, special education teachers, support staff and support staff administration?
7. Is there coordination and priority setting among possible competing programs such as curriculum implementation, building-based instructional improvement projects, employee assistance programs, wellness programs, general professional growth courses, and programs that respond to high-priority areas such as substance abuse prevention, child abuse, neglect, or other legal mandates?
8. To what extent does the district's staff development program exemplify a contemporary view of staff development as described in the Introduction?
9. Following are indicators of an institutionalized staff development function in a school district. How many of the following are part of the local program?
   * Clearly stated set of beliefs regarding staff development.
   * Some type of written staff development policy.
   * Full- or part-time district staff position accountable for the staff development programs.
   * Line item budget support for staff development.
   * Procedures and guidelines for awarding credit and other aspects of staff development.
   * Processes for gathering input on staff development needs from all segments of the staff and decision makers.
   * A norm of lifelong learning for all staff.
   * An application of the research base in adult learning and change applied to all staff development programs and activities.

incentives and rewards (see Cheerleading, below). Some large districts have their own grant programs that permit individuals, groups, or schools to apply for district funds to support local improvement efforts. Large districts may also support a staff development academy to train teachers and administrators to serve as district trainers and consultants. A district-level budget may pay for teachers or administrators to attend out-of-district conferences or training programs in order to bring specific skills back to the district.

"Cheerleading"

Staff development takes time, energy, and resources, and people involved in change efforts need ongoing support and encouragement. The staff developer has a crucial role to play in cheering on as well as leading participants in change efforts.

One popular cheerleading strategy is a district staff development newsletter that focuses on all three levels of staff development: individual, school-based, and districtwide. A newsletter can not only highlight effective practices throughout the district but can also give visibility and credibility to individuals, groups, and schools that are engaging in substantive improvement efforts. (Such newsletters perform a linking service by listing district-sponsored and out-of-district staff development activities.)

Districts have their own grant programs that permit individuals, groups, or schools to apply for district funds to support local improvement efforts.

Other district cheerleading strategies include reward and recognition programs such as Distinguished Teacher, Teacher of the Month/Year, mini-grants, mini-sabbaticals, or adjunct professorships at neighboring universities. Arranging for out-of-district guests may be time-consuming for staff developers, but such visits often provide payoffs in increased satisfaction and professional self-esteem, and boost morale in the district if described in the staff development newsletter. The staff developer's presence in schools and classrooms can also have a cheerleading effect provided the staff developer does not serve in an evaluative capacity.

Summary

Specifically, then, the essential function of district-level staff developers is to provide:
* Written staff development philosophy, policies, and procedures.
* A system for gathering input on the needs of staff members and decision makers.
* A structure for providing district-level programs.
* Staff members who are accountable for district-level programs
* Line-item budget support.
* Procedures and guidelines for earning course credit.
* Support for non-district-level staff development activities.
* Information about district and other staff development opportunities.

Organization of District Staff Development Programs

Organizational structure can be determined by specific programs or by the defined roles and responsibilities of participants.

Program-Based Organization

Although no one organizational model can take into account all the possible components of district staff development, one example can serve as a starting point. Reported by Sparks and Schiff (1986) and shown in Figure 1.3, this model includes:

* A curriculum function involving direct support of all phases of curriculum development, including identifying needs, piloting programs, field testing, districtwide implementation, and evaluation.
* An instruction function for developing, adapting, and delivering staff training activities to help teachers and administrators expand their repertoire of teaching and classroom management strategies.
* A quality-of-worklife and organizational development function supported by leadership training and management development, and providing the services of a highly-trained cadre of in-house process consultants.

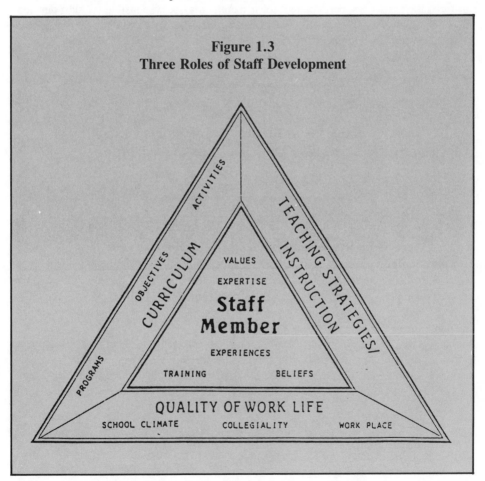

Figure 1.3
Three Roles of Staff Development

Such a structure might call for district-level curriculum coordinators or department chairs supervised by an assistant superintendent to provide the curriculum development function with a staff developer responsible for the staff development aspects of all three functions.

Client-Based Organization

Because staff development focuses on developing human resources within the district, another appropriate way to organize staff development is in terms of client needs. Organization focuses on three kinds of programs for different clients:

* Certified staff — new teachers, experienced teachers, counselors, school psychologists and social workers, special education teachers and related staff members, and administrators.
* Support staff — secretaries, instructional and teacher aides, bookkeepers, custodians, food-service and transportation workers, and classified administrators.
* Non-employees — parents, law enforcement officials, citizen committee members, and board of education members.

Under such an organizational structure, one central office administrator may be responsible for all three kinds of programs, or responsibilities may be divided. In large districts, the assistant superintendent for personnel may be responsible for staff development for support staff, while the assistant superintendent for curriculum and instruction coordinates staff development for certified staff.

The staff developer has a crucial role to play in cheering on as well as leading participants in change efforts.

Responsibility for Staff Development

Whatever the organizational structure, responsibility for staff development may be assumed by people in several roles. In districts with less than 5,000 students, for example, staff development is usually provided solely by principals and teachers on special assignment, either part-time or full-time for short periods, overseen by the assistant superintendent or by the superintendent.

In larger districts, duties are often differentiated by placing part of the staff development program in curriculum and instruction and part in personnel. When this occurs, coordination between the two departments is essential so that all populations are adequately served and so that the kinds of training provided each client group supports the work of teachers in the classroom.

Districts larger than 25,000 students present more complex possibilities. With their multiple resources and multiple layers of administrative control, large districts face the challenge of maintaining a balance between centralizing staff development to increase efficiency and decentralizing it to produce more personal involvement.

A comprehensive staff development program in a large district would include the following fulltime and/or part time professional positions:
* Managers or coordinators.
* Trainers, instructors, facilitators.
* Process consultants.
* Trainers of trainers.
* Course and workshop developers.
* Researchers/analysts.

See Figure 1.4 for a list of competencies for these managers or coordinators. In small districts many or all of these services may be purchased as needed from outside consultants. Whatever the district size, some responsibilities may be combined and others may be distributed outside the staff development office to increase the talent pool and to develop strong personal involvement and commitment throughout the organization.

The school district ultimately bears responsibility for providing an effective staff development program on every level. Designing and maintaining a comprehensive, diversified, and goal-focused program is a challenge for those involved in mature as well as in fledgling staff development programs.

Figure 1.4
Competencies

This chapter deals with the general district organization for staff development. Therefore, the skills needed are those needed by a district level staff development administrator/manager/leader.

Planning Skills
1. Problem/need/issues identification skills.
2. Ability to develop a vision of what the future program will look like and to share that vision through oral and written communication.
3. Knowledge of strategic planning strategies.
4. Ability to develop a course syllabus.
5. Ability to involve many different groups of people in the planning process.

Organizing Skills
1. Ability to organize the entire effort of staff development into workable parts. This includes being able to write job descriptions for full-time and part-time employees and being able to hire appropriate personnel for these various roles.
2. Identifying and brokering human resource talent from district staff members and outside consultants.
3. Establishing formal linkages within the district's organizational structure to include the staff development function.

(Fig. 4, cont.)

Monitoring and Evaluating Skills
1. Formal evaluation design and methodology.
2. Personnel performance appraisal and evaluation.
3. Organizational development and climate monitoring and evaluation.
4. Conferencing and giving feedback.

Financial Management Skills
1. Basic financial mathematics.
2. Basic understanding of accounting procedures.
3. Working knowledge of district's budgeting process or the ability to establish an unique budget process for staff development.

Communication Skills
1. Written communication through memos, letters, reports and scheduling documents.
2. Interpersonal communication.
3. Large-group presentation.
4. Spokesperson communication.
5. Group facilitation.

Content Expertise
1. Should be an acknowledged expert/trainer in at least two or three areas of instruction, management, and training of trainers.
2. Should be knowledgeable of research-based effective practices in teaching, supervision, staff development.

References

Combs, A.W., & Avila, D.L. (1985). *Helping relationships: Basic concepts for the helping professions* (3rd ed.). Boston: Allyn and Bacon.

Sparks, G., & Schiff, S. (1986, May). The triangle model of staff development. *The Developer*, 1, 7.

Large districts face the challenge of maintaining a balance between centralizing staff development to increase efficiency and decentralizing it to produce more personal involvement.

Chapter 2

Organizing and Managing School-Based Staff Development

No significant improvement in administration, teaching, or school programs can occur without effective staff development. Conversely, staff development is aimless and ineffective without clearly defined improvement goals aimed at increasing school effectiveness.

Fred H. Wood

For more than two decades, research has indicated that the school should be the focus of efforts to improve educational practice (Gross & Herriott, 1965). Many teachers and administrators intuitively have come to the same conclusion — that the school is the primary unit of change in education. No matter how much effort is put into districtwide improvement programs, some schools in the district will improve and others will not.

This realization was one impetus for research on effective schools conducted in the 1970s. These studies confirm that the school, not the district, is the unit of change when increased student achievement is the goal (Brookover et al., 1979; Edmunds, 1979; Perkey & Smith, 1982). Goodlad's 1984 study of schooling in the United States also clearly identifies the school as the legitimate target of change and improvement.

Such research has focused increased attention on both school improvement and staff development. This dual focus is appropriate because the two are interdependent. No significant improvement in administration, teaching, or school programs can occur without effective staff development. Conversely, staff development is aimless and ineffective without clearly identified improvement goals aimed at increasing school effectiveness.

In the previous chapter, Metzdorf points out that staff development occurs at several levels within a school district. Some problems and issues are districtwide and must be addressed by district-level staff development. Other staff development needs are related to the personal/professional growth of individual teachers and administrators (see Chapter 3). Finally, some needs require school-based staff development.

School-Based Staff Development Assumptions and Practices

Researchers have discovered a great deal about effective staff development practices during the last two decades. Emerging from the literature on professional attitudes and perceptions of staff development, change process, organizational development, adult learning, effective training practice in education and business, leadership behavior, and, most recently, effective schools is a new set of assumptions and practices that supports school-based staff development (Thompson, 1982; Wood et al., 1981) and may lead to improved professional development programs. These assumptions are:

* The school, not the district, is the primary unit of change (Berman & McLaughlin, 1978; Goodlad, 1984; Henderson & Perry, 1981).
* Significant change in educational practice takes considerable time and is the result of long-range staff development programs conducted for three to five years (Crandall, 1983).
* A positive, healthy school climate that includes trust, open communication, and peer support for changes in practice is essential for successful staff development (Chamberlin, 1971; Zagarmi, 1981).
* Those who are changing their behavior must make personal and group commitments to the new practices or programs so that they will want to participate in and learn from inservice activities (Berman & Pauley, 1975; Sparks, 1983).
* The principal is the key to facilitating improvement in the school (Behling, 1981; Curran, 1982; Kelley, 1981; Miller, 1982; Shoemaker & Fraser, 1981).
* All school personnel should be involved in staff development throughout their professional lives (Rubin, 1971).
* Staff development should focus on helping school personnel improve job performance (Wood & Thompson, 1981).
* As adult learners, educators are motivated to learn when individual differences are recognized and when educators have some control over what and how they learn (Withall & Wood, 1979).
* Learning by doing is an important component of an adult learning program (Arends et al., 1980; Lawrence, 1974; Roy, 1987).

* Leadership in designing and implementing staff development should be shared by administrators and learners (Sparks, 1983).
* The purpose of staff development is to improve professional practice and student achievement (Wood et al., 1982).
* The cost of staff development for improved practice should be paid by the school district (Wood et al., 1981).

Designing a School-Based Staff Development Program

To systematically plan and implement inservice programs that respond to school-based improvement goals, research and effective practice suggest five stages.

* **Readiness.** Faculty members study, select, and make a commitment to new behaviors and programs that focus on improving professional practice and student achievement.
* **Planning.** Faculty members develop long-range plan to achieve the changes identified in the first stage.
* **Training.** Inservice training sessions are conducted based upon what is known about adult learners.
* **Implementation.** Participants integrate new professional behaviors and knowledge into daily work activities with follow-up assistance.
* **Maintenance.** Changes in practice are monitored to ensure continued high levels of performance.

A positive, healthy school climate that includes trust, open communication, and peer support for changes in practice is essential for successful staff development.

These stages and the 38 practices (see Figure 2.1) that define them are supported by research (Thompson, 1982; Wood et al., 1982). Each stage identifies specific issues that staff developers need to address as they plan and implement school-based staff development.

Readiness Activities

At the readiness stage, faculty members, with assistance from staff developers and central-office administrators, need to:

* Examine the major problems of the district and their school and become familiar with the newest and most promising ideas, practices, and trends in education — in short, define what is needed and what is possible (Wood et al., 1985).
* Develop a school climate in which faculty members know each other well, have clarified their educational values, support open communication, have the skills for group decision making and problem solving, see the strengths in diversity among their peers, and support colleagues who are making changes in their professional practice (Berman & McLaughlin, 1978; Comer, 1980; Schienfield, 1979).

Figure 2.1
RPTIM Model Practices

Stage I: Readiness

1. A positive school climate is developed before other staff development efforts are attempted.
2. Goals for school improvement are written collaboratively by teachers, parents, building administrators, and central office administrators.
3. The school has a written list of goals for the improvement of school programs during the next three to five years.
4. The school staff adopts and supports goals for the improvement of school programs.
5. Current school practices are examined to determine which ones are congruent with the school's goals for improvement before staff development activities are planned.
6. Current educational practices not yet found in the school are examined to determine which ones are congruent with the school's goals for improvement before staff development activities are planned.
7. The school staff identifies specific plans to achieve the school's goals for improvement.
8. Leadership and support during the initial stage of staff development activity are the responsibility of the principal and central office staff.

Stage II: Planning

9. Differences between desired and actual practices in the school are examined to identify the inservice needs of the staff.
10. Planning of staff development activities relies, in part, on information gathered directly from school staff members.
11. Inservice planners use information about the learning styles of participants when planning staff development activities.
12. Staff development programs include objectives for inservice activities covering as much as five years.
13. The resources available for use in staff development are identified prior to planning inservice activities.
14. Staff development programs include plans for activities to be conducted during the following three to five years.
15. Specific objectives are written for staff development activities.
16. Staff development objectives include objectives for attitude development (new outlooks and feelings).
17. Staff development objectives include objectives for increased knowledge (new information and understanding).
18. Staff development objectives include objectives for skill development (new work behaviors).
19. Leadership during the planning of inservice programs is shared among teachers and administrators.

(Fig. 2.1, cont.)

Stage III: Training

20. Staff development activities include the use of learning teams in which two to seven participants share and discuss learning experiences.
21. Individual school staff members choose objectives for their own professional learning.
22. Individual school staff members choose the staff development activities in which they participate.
23. Staff development activities include experiential activities in which participants try out new behaviors and techniques.
24. Peers help to teach one another by serving as inservice leaders.
25. School principals participate in staff development activities with their staffs.
26. Leaders of staff development activities are selected according to their expertise rather than their position.
27. As participants in staff development activities become increasingly competent, leadership behavior becomes less directive or task-oriented.
28. As participants in staff development activities become increasingly confident in their abilities, the leader transfers increasing responsibility to the participants.

Stage IV: Implementation

29. After participating in inservice activities, participants have access to support services to help implement new behaviors as part of their regular work.
30. School staff members who attempt to implement new learnings are recognized for their efforts.
31. The leaders of staff development activities visit the job setting, when needed, to help the inservice participants refine or review previous learning.
32. School staff members use peer supervision to assist one another in implementing new work behaviors.
33. Resources are allocated to support the implementation of new practices following staff development activities (funds to purchase new instructional materials, time for planning, and so forth).
34. The school principal actively supports efforts to implement changes in professional behavior.

Stage V: Maintenance

35. A systematic program of instructional supervision is used to monitor new work behavior.
36. School staff members utilize systematic techniques of self-monitoring to maintain new work behaviors.
37. Student feedback is used to monitor new practices.
38. Responsibility for the maintenance of new school practices is shared by both teachers and administrators.

Source: *Leader's Guide, Effective Teaching for Higher Achievement* (Alexandria, VA: Association for Supervision and Curriculum Development, 1984), 4-5.

* Collaboratively develop — with the help of parents, community leaders, and central-office representatives — a written set of three- to five-year goals for school improvement that are support by the teachers and principal (Berman & McLaughlin, 1978; Lawrence, 1974; Litwin & Stringer, 1968).
* Examine practices and programs inside and outside the school to determine which are congruent with the staff's improvement goals (Caldwell & Wood, 1981).
* Select practices and programs that faculty members will implement to achieve their improvement goals over the next three to five years (Berman & McLaughlin, 1978).

At the readiness stage, examine the major problems of the district and their school and become familiar with the newest and most promising ideas, practices, and trends in education.

Planning Activities

Once the goals and programs or practices are selected, faculty members and administrators share responsibility for planning. In this stage, those responsible for staff development should work with the principal and teachers to:

* Identify the specific practices that teachers, principals, parents, and students will need to demonstrate when the improvement goals and programs are implemented (Charters & Jones, 1974).
* Conduct a needs assessment to determine the extent to which the desired practices are present in their school (Charters & Jones, 1974; Dillon-Peterson & Hammer, 1980; Oja, 1980; Rubin, 1978).
* Determine the resources available to support staff development programs and personnel during the current budget year and during the next three to five years (Wood et al., 1981).
* Develop detailed, written plans for staff development that include:
  - Knowledge, skills, and attitude objectives required to achieve the three- to five-year school improvement goals,
  - Detailed first-year inservice training activities to achieve the short-range goals of the plan,
  - General training activities for each of the remaining years of the plan, and
  - Strategies to get and keep support and approval of the written plan, including a budget agreed on by the school faculty, central office, and the board of education (Dillon-Peterson & Greenewald, 1980; Havelock & Havelock, 1973; Rubin, 1978; Sarason, 1971; Sergiovanni, 1979).

Training Activities

In the training stage, staff development plans are implemented to help faculty members learn new skills and knowledge and to develop attitudes needed to achieve improvement goals. Workshops should reflect what is known about adult learning. This is the stage that has traditionally been called inservice education.

Research suggests that inservice activities should:

* Present a rationale based on both theory and research in addition to the "nuts and bolts" of what is to be learned (Sparks, 1983).
* Use small-group or team learning when higher-order thinking and a secure learning environment are desired (Institute for the Development of Educational Activities, 1971; Johnson & Johnson, 1980; Tough, 1967).
* Provide choices in objectives and activities so that participants have some control over their own learning (Dillon-Peterson & Hammer, 1980; Massey, 1980; Roy, 1987).
* Involve participants in directed practice so they can try out new behaviors, techniques, and ideas and get helpful feedback (Arends et al., 1980; Joyce & Showers, 1980; Lawrence, 1974; Wood & Neil, 1976).
* Use teachers and administrators with appropriate expertise as inservice leaders (Rubin, 1978).
* Have the principal participate with teachers and have the superintendent participate with principals (Berman & McLaughlin, 1978; Hall et al., 1982).
* Complete, share, and critique action plans for using what is learned once the participant is back on the job (Wood et al., 1982).

Develop detailed, written plans for staff development that include objectives, activities, strategies to get and keep support, and a budget.

Implementation Activities

A major challenge for staff development programs is ensuring that what is learned in inservice finds its way into the day-to-day work activities of participants. This is the stage at which the teachers and principals must make the transition from learning in the controlled setting of inservice training to adjusting and adapting what they have learned to make it part of their daily work activities. During implementation, faculty members completing inservice training should be provided follow-up assistance including:

* Planned visits to the work site by the staff development trainer (Joyce & Showers, 1982).
* On-call or scheduled peer observations and meetings to provide feedback, share experiences, and solve problems (Buckley, 1975; Goldsberry, 1980; Joyce & Showers, 1982; Lawrence, 1974; Little, 1981).

* Access to resources supporting implementation, such as materials, release time to plan or modify plans, and personnel to provide on-site coaching (Berman & McLaughlin, 1978; Little, 1981).
* Recognition, rewards, and assistance for those implementing their new learning from administrators, especially from immediate supervisors (Dillon-Peterson & Hammer, 1980; Little, 1981).

In the training stage, involve participants in directed practice so they can try out new behaviors, techniques, and ideas and get helpful feedback.

Maintenance Activities

At this stage, professional behaviors being used in daily classroom and school practice are monitored to ensure their continuation. Teachers and administrators share responsibility for maintaining the quality of practices and programs that have been learned through inservice training and installed through coaching on the job. Maintenance activities should include:

* Systematic supervision by school and district administrators (Berman & McLaughlin, 1978).
* Systematic consultation with colleagues so teachers and administrators can provide feedback to their peers (Goldsberry, 1980).
* Collection of feedback related to practice used or not used from students and parents (Wood et al., 1981).

These five stages describe practices in many school-based improvement programs. For example, the model school-based staff development and improvement programs presented in *Reaching for Excellence: Effective School Handbook* (Kyle, 1985) make extensive use of the practices that define these five stages. Programs that appear to address all five stages include the School Improvement Program (SIP), developed by the California State Department of Education; the Effective School Program, developed by the Mid-Continent Regional Education Laboratory; the District School Improvement Program, developed by the Detroit Public Schools; Project SHAL, developed by the St. Louis Public Schools; and the Pittsburgh School Improvement Program, developed by the Pittsburgh Public Schools. The Minnesota Plan for School Effectiveness, designed by the Minnesota Department of Education, uses most of these practices (Roy et al., 1986). The School Improvement Process, developed by the Institute for the Development of Educational Activities (I/D/E/A/), was specifically designed to address all 38 practices in the 5 stages.

Although each district and school is different, and the procedures used to implement school-based staff development must reflect those differences, the research-based practices presented here should be considered carefully by all districts moving toward school-based improvement.

Validation of the Five Stages

The practices that define these five stages of school-based staff development were identified through an extensive review of research related to staff development (Thompson, 1982). Then a national study was conducted to determine whether experts with extensive experience in staff development would support this approach to designing professional development programs (Wood et al., 1982). While the results showed that professors and practitioners strongly supported all 38 practices, the following practices were perceived as essential:

* Develop a positive school climate.
* Have three- to five-year improvement goals.
* Have the faculty adopt and support school improvement goals.
* Involve the faculty in selecting programs to achieve improvement goals.
* Conduct needs assessments.
* Know the available resources before planning staff development programs.
* Share leadership for planning inservice training.
* Have the principal participate in inservice training with teachers.
* Select inservice trainers for their expertise.
* Provide follow-up coaching.
* Have the principal recognize and support those who implement changes.

A major challenge for staff development programs is ensuring that what is learned in inservice finds its way into the day-to-day work activities of participants.

The same study revealed that all 38 practices were neglected in current staff development programs. The findings pointed out that readiness, implementation, and maintenance were the most neglected stages. The most neglected practices included:

* Developing a positive school climate.
* Collaborating in the development of school improvement goals.
* Setting three- to five-year improvement goals.
* Examining current practice in the school.
* Conducting needs assessments.
* Providing follow-up assistance.
* Having the principal recognize those implementing changes.
* Making sure adequate resources for implementation were available.
* Using self-monitoring and student feedback to ensure maintenance.
* Sharing responsibility for maintenance among teachers and administrators.

It appears that there is strong support for this school-based approach. This support is found throughout the literature and in four studies conducted to test the five stages (Delgado-Albino, 1983; McQuarrie, 1984; Thompson, 1982; Wood et al., 1982). This approach gives us a view of what schools need to do to achieve school-based improvement. However, it does not explain what a district needs to do to implement school-based staff development and improvement.

Districtwide Staff Development
for School-Based Improvement

Districts implementing school-based improvement have had difficulty moving from a centralized to a decentralized system of change. Such a move requires major modifications in the way staff developers and others in the district behave and think.

In the initial stages of transferring primary responsibility for improvement to the school, certain questions need to be asked:

* What organization is required for successful school-based change?
* What should be the role and mission of staff development in this context?
* What staff development practices are most appropriate to school-based improvement?
* How should staff development be organized and managed to facilitate school-based improvement goals and plans?
* What training programs will be necessary for central office personnel, principals, and staff developers as the district enters school-based improvements?

Two case studies in large districts moving toward school-based change have provided some of the answers to these questions, at least for the early stages of implementing school-based improvement (Wood et al., 1984; Wood & Thompson, 1985; Wood et al., 1986). Most information in the following section is based on results of these studies.

Teachers and administrators share responsibility for maintaining the quality of practices and programs that have been learned through inservice training and installed through coaching on the job.

Context for School-Based Change

The process begins with the board of education selecting 10 to 15 improvement goals that address the major educational problems in the district. The central office then establishes procedures for faculty members to select three to six of the district improvement goals and the programs to achieve them. Using data for their schools provided by the central office, principals guide faculty members and community representatives through this selection process. This group writes a five-year improvement plan for achieving school goals. Than plan is reviewed and approved by the central office and board of education.

After approval, the school starts implementation through staff development. At this point, the district administrators turn their efforts to supporting and facilitating the implementation of the school-level plans. District administrators also monitor and provide feedback about progress toward school improvement goals to the school staff members and to the board of education.

During this process, the roles of the board of education, central office staff, and school faculty each change substantially. For example, the board of education must refocus on establishing policies that support differences rather than uniformity among schools. The board also must identify improvement goals that focus on the major educational problems facing the district, monitor progress toward district goals through improvements in each school, and serve as an advocate for the school improvement process.

The central office no longer is totally responsible for deciding the who, what, how, and when of change. Decisions about which specific improvements are to be implemented in schools should be made by faculty members in each school. The central office management team facilitates rather than directs this decision. Top district administrators identify procedures as well as provide and manage resources that enable principals and their teachers to implement improvement plans.

Of course, central office administrators decide whether plans developed at the school level are appropriate and congruent with district goals. They also monitor schools' progress toward their goals, and they are responsible for evaluating the impact of school plans on student achievement and professional practice. This shift in emphasis from directing and telling to providing services and support is quite a change from common practice.

The principal's primary role is to plan and implement school improvement. The principal has much more control over staff members, budget, and inservice education. Teachers have more control over the improvement goals and programs they will pursue in their school and over the design, instructors, and evaluation of their inservice education.

Moving from a centralized to a decentralized system of change requires major modifications in the way staff developers and others in the district behave and think.

Roles and Mission of Staff Development

In this approach to decentralized change, staff developers place primary emphasis on:
* Helping principals develop improvement plans for their schools.
* Working with principals to plan and deliver inservice programs that focus on school-based improvement goals.
* Planning, delivering, and managing inservice training that enables district-level administrators to carry out their roles in school-based change.
* Assisting in the evaluation of inservice training.
* Coordinating district staff development activities.
* Establishing a link between school improvement, staff development, and personnel evaluation.

The key words for staff developers should be "respond," "support," and "assist" as they work with district personnel to improve professional practice and student achievement. For principals, this means help in developing school improvement goals and plans and in planning and implementing inservice training for their faculty. For central office administrators, this means assistance as they make the transition from directors and final decision makers to facilitators of decisions made at the school level.

Practices to Support School-Based
Staff Development

A crucial decision as districts move into school-based change is selecting a systematic, research-based process for planning and implementing school-based staff development. The first part of this chapter describes a five-stage staff development model. Two other staff development models that support school improvement are described by Loucks-Horsley and Hergert (1985) and Sparks et al. (1985).

Organization and Management of
School-Based Staff Development

Although decisions about change and staff development are made at the school level, a districtwide staff development program still is needed. It is impossible for each school to have the expertise and resources to implement its inservice plans. (Metzdorf addresses this issue in Chapter 1.)

One major misconception about school-based staff development and improvement is that all inservice training occurs in the school. Staff development may be school-based and yet

The key words for staff developers should be "respond," "support," and "assist" as they work with district personnel to improve professional practice and student achievement.

be offered outside the school in a district training center or in a graduate class at a university. Staff development is school-based when participants address one of their own school's goals; place is less important than the nature and goals of the training activity.

Districts with several schools planning staff development for school-by-school improvement should consider:

* Establishing a district unit or department for staff development, directed by an administrator.
* Identifying personnel to coordinate inservice education for administrators, teachers, and school improvement planning.
* Housing all personnel with major responsibility for staff development in a single building to help them coordinate, communicate, and focus their efforts on school-based goals.
* Establishing a staff development council for the district to promote coordinated inservice activities, cooperation, and efficient use of limited resources.
* Identifying staff development funds, inservice programs, and trainers available inside and outside the district that are related to the district's improvement goals.
* Developing a computerized catalog of the staff development resources related to the district's improvement goals so principals and staff developers will have easy access to the assistance they need (Caldwell & Marshall, 1982).

Training Programs Needed

Any time a district attempts to make major changes in current practice, the need for staff development increases. Thus, the move to school-based improvement will require special inservice programs for boards of education, central office administrators, principals, teachers, and staff developers. The inservice training needs during the early years of school-based staff development vary depending on the audience.

Boards of education need inservice training that enables them to:

1. Understand the rationale for school-based change.
2. Identify and revise policy to support school-based improvement.
3. Select district improvement goals.
4. Interpret evaluation data related to district improvement goals.
5. Understand the impact of school-based improvement on the roles of central office staff, principals, and teachers.

Central office personnel need inservice training that enables them to:

1. Understand the impact of school-based improvement on their roles and responsibilities.
2. Learn to facilitate school-level improvement.
3. Work as an effective management team.
4. Determine which decisions and tasks should be centralized and which should be school-based.
5. Guide schools through at least one process of site-based goal setting and planning.

Principals need inservice training that enables them to:

1. Use effective communication and interpersonal skills.
2. Use at least one systematic process to plan and implement school improvement.
3. Understand, model, and identify effective instructional practices.
4. Use district staff development resources and personnel.
5. Establish a colleague support group with other principals to share resources, solve problems, and help each other with school improvement projects.

Teachers need inservice training that enables them to:

1. Collaborate with the principal in decisions about improvement goals and programs.
2. Employ effective teaching practices related to increased student learning in the areas of classroom management, discipline, direct instruction, time on task, mastery learning, and higher-order thinking.
3. Serve as peer instructors and coaches in their school or districtwide inservice programs.

Finally, *staff developers* need inservice training that enables them to:

1. Work as an effective staff development team by developing skills in group process, consensus seeking, and problem solving.
2. Use at least one systematic process to plan and implement school improvement.
3. Work with principals to plan and conduct inservice training that addresses the improvement needs and goals of the schools.
4. Design or choose effective staff development programs.

These staff development needs identify some, but not all, or the initial training needs of school personnel when the district targets the school as the unit of change. There are certainly other inservice needs, but they will have to be discovered through more experience with and research on decentralized school improvement.

Figure 2.2
Competencies

1. Plan and conduct activities and programs to develop positive school climate.
2. Design and conduct team building and goal setting activities for a school staff.
3. Assist school faculty members in selecting programs and practices to achieve school improvement goals.
4. Assist principals and teachers in the collaborative development of a three- to five-year improvement plan consistent with available resources.
5. Design, adapt, and select inservice training programs that are consistent with the research on adult learning.
6. Design follow-up support systems for implementing new practices on the job after inservice training.
7. Identify specific practices that build ownership and commitment to improved practice through the five stages of the RPTIM staff development process.
8. Identify the role of supervision in effective staff development.
9. Build staff development programs that reflect the relationship between supervision, teacher evaluation, and inservice training.
10. Assist others in the design of "action plans" for implementing the results of inservice training.
11. Plan staff development programs using at least one research-based model for school-based staff development.
12. Design and implement districtwide staff development programs that are consistent with the research on effective staff development programs.
13. Describe the changes needed in the typical district to accommodate school-based improvement through staff development (i.e., changes in roles, decision making procedures, staff development programs, and curriculum).

Summary

Staff development research indicates that staff developers need to address these questions as they move toward decentralized, school-based staff improvement.

1. Have the board of education and superintendent made a reasoned commitment to school-by-school improvement and the assumptions that support effective staff development?
2. Has the district identified procedures that will be used to plan and implement school-based improvement and staff development?
3. Have the new roles required by school-based improvement been identified for the board of education, central office administrators, principals, teachers, and staff development personnel?
4. Has the mission of staff development been redefined to support school-based improvement?
5. Have principals and other school personnel been prepared to use systematic procedures for planning and implementing school-based staff development programs based on these five stages: readiness, planning, training, implementation, and maintenance?

6. Has a staff development unit been established that coordinates and manages resources and inservice programs for the district?
7. Have inservice training programs been established and implemented to prepare the board of education, central office personnel, principals, and teachers for their new responsibilities for school-based change?
8. Have staff developers redefined their role so they can provide the services and programs required to achieve district improvement goals?

If the answer to each question is yes, you are well on your way to implementing school-based staff development. If not, you now have the information necessary to move from centralized to decentralized improvement and professional development.

A crucial decision as districts move into school-based change is selecting a systematic, research-based process for planning and implementing school-based staff development.

References

Arends, R., Hersh, R., & Turner, J. (1908). *Conditions for promoting effective staff development*. Washington, DC: ERIC Clearinghouse on Teacher Education.

Behling, H.E., Jr. (1981). *What recent research says about effective schools and effective classrooms*. Chelonsford, MD: Update Northeastern Region Exchange.

Berman, P., & McLaughlin, S. (1978). *Implementing and sustaining innovation*. Vol. 8 of *Federal programs supporting educational change*. Santa Monica, CA: Rand Corporation.

Berman, P., & Pauley, E.W. *Factors affecting change agent projects*. Vol. 2 of *Federal programs supporting educational changes*. Santa Monica, CA: Rand Corporation.

Brookover, W.B., & Lezotte, L. (1979). *Changes in schools' characteristics coincident with changes in student achievement. Occasional paper No. 17*. East Lansing, MI: Institute for Research on Teaching, Michigan State University.

Brookover, W.B., Beady, C., Flood, P., Schwertzer, J., & Wesenbaker, J. (1979). *School systems and student achievement*. New York: Praeger.

Buckely, J.J., Jr. (1975, May). Peer supervision improves teacher's interaction in a non-threatening atmosphere. *Education Summary*.

Caldwell, S.D., & Marshall, J. (1982, April). Information, management and evaluation of staff development. *Journal of Staff Development*, 84-101.

Caldwell, S.D., & Wood, F.H. (1981, June). Inservice readiness: Do we have the cart before the horse? *The Developer*, 1-5.

Chamberlin, L.J. (1971). *Effective instruction through dynamic discipline*. Columbus, OH: Charles E. Merrill.

Charters, W.W., & Jones, J.E. (1974). *On neglect of the independent variable in program evaluation. Project MITT Occasional Paper.* Eugene, OR: Center for Educational Policy and Management, University of Oregon.

Comer, J. (1980). The education of inner city children. *Grants Magazine, 1,* 20-26.

Crandall, D. (1983, Nov.). The teacher's role in school improvement. *Educational Leadership, 41*(3), 6-9.

Curran, E.A. (1982). If the object is learning? *American Education, 18,* 15-18.

Delgado-Albino, A.M. (1983). *A survey and analysis of Puerto Rico accredited institutions of higher education personnel perceptions of faculty development practices and beliefs with a view to identifying some critical needs.* Doctoral dissertation, The Pennsylvania State University.

Dillon-Peterson, B., & Greenewald, G. (1980). *Staff development for the social studies teacher.* Boulder, CO: ERIC Clearinghouse for Social Studies/Social Science Education.

Dillon-Peterson, B., & Hammer, C. (1980, Nov.). Applications of adult learning through staff development. *Journal of Staff Development, 1,* 79-87.

Edmunds, R.R. (1979, Oct.). Effective schools for the urban poor. *Educational Leadership, 37,* 15-27.

Goldsberry, L.F. (1980). *Colleague consultation: Teacher collaboration, using a clinical supervision method.* Doctoral dissertation, University of Illinois-Champaign.

Goodlad, J.I. (1984). *A place called school.* New York: McGraw-Hill.

Gross, N., & Herriott, R.E. (1965). *Staff leadership in public schools: A sociological inquiry.* New York: Wiley.

Hall, G.E., Rutherford, W.C., & Griffin, T.H. (1982). *Three change factor styles: Some indicators and a proposed framework.* Austin, TX: R & D Report No. 3134.

Havelock, E., & Havelock, M.C. (1973). *Training for change agents: A guide to the designs of training programs in education and other fields.* Ann Arbor, MI: Institute for Social Research, University of Michigan.

Henderson, E., & Perry, G. (1981). *Change and development in schools.* London: McGraw-Hill.

Institute for the Development of Educational Activities. (1971). *Learning in small groups.* Dayton, OH: Author.

Johnson, D. & Johnson, R. (1980, Nov.). The key to effective inservice: Building teacher-teacher collaboration. *The Developer,* 1-4.

Joyce, B., & Peck, L. (1977). *Inservice teacher education project report II: Interviews.* Syracuse, NY: Syracuse University.

Joyce, B., & Showers, B. (1980, Feb.). Improving inservice training: The message of research. *Educational Leadership, 37,* 379-385.

Joyce, B., & Showers, B. (1982, Oct.). The coaching of teaching. *Educational Leadership, 40,* 4-10.

Kelley, E.A. (1981, Dec.). Auditing school climates. *Educational Leadership, 39,* 180-183.

Kyle, R.M.J., Ed. (1985). *Reaching for excellence: An effective schools sourcebook.* Washington, DC: U.S. Government Printing Office.

Lawrence, G. (1974). *Patterns of effective inservice education: Review of research.* Tallahassee, FL: Florida State Department of Education.

Little, J.W. (1981). *School success and staff development: The role of staff development in urban desegregated schools.* Boulder, CO: Center for Action Research.

Litwin, G., & Stringer, R., Jr. (1968). *Motivation and organizational climate.* Cambridge, MA: Harvard University.

Loucks-Horsely, S., & Hergert, L. (1985). *An action guide to school improvement.* Alexandria, VA: Association for Supervision and Curriculum development/The Network.

Massey, S.R. (1980, Nov.). Teaching adult professionals. *Journal of Staff Development, 1,* 88-96.

McQuarrie, F.O., Wood, F.H., & Thompson, S.R. (1984, Feb.). The staff development maze: Where are we? *NASSP Bulletin, 68,* 75-82.

Miller, S.K. (1982, Dec.). School learning climate improvement. *Educational Leadership, 40,* 36-37.

Oja, S.N. (1980, Nov.). Adult development is implicit in staff development. *Journal of Staff Development, 1,* 7-56.

Perkey, S., & Smith, M. (1982). *Effective school — A review.* Madison, WI: Wisconsin Center for Education Research, School of Education, University of Wisconsin at Madison.

Roy, P. (1987, Fall). Consumer's guide to selecting staff development consultants. *The Developer, 2,* 8-9.

Roy, P.A., Mesenburg, R.J., & Lillesve, M. (1986, May). The Minnesota plan for school effectiveness. *Journal of Staff Development, 2,* 18-28.

Rubin, L.J. (1978). The case for staff development. In T.J. Sergiovanni (Ed.), *Professional supervision for professional teachers.* Alexandria, VA: Association for Supervision and Curriculum Development.

Rubin, L.J. (1971). *Inservice education of teachers: Trends, processes, and prescriptions.* Boston, MA: Allyn and Bacon.

Sarason, S. (1971). *The culture of the school and the problem of change.* Boston, MA: Allyn and Bacon.

Schienfield, D.A. (1979, Feb.). A three-faceted design for renewing elementary schools. *Theory Into Practice, 1B,* 114-125.

Sergiovanni, T.J. (1979). *Supervision: Human perspectives.* New York: McGraw-Hill.

Shoemaker, J., & Fraser, H.W. (1981). What principals can do: Some implications from studies of effective schooling. *Phi Delta Kappan, 63,* 178-182.

Sparks, G. (1983, Nov.). Synthesis of research on staff development for effective teaching. *Educational Leadership, 41*(3), 65-72.

Sparks, G., Nowakowski, M., Hall, B., Allec, R., & Imrick, J. (1985, March). School improvement through staff development. *Educational Leadership, 42,* 59-61.

Thompson, S.R. (1982). *A survey and analysis of Pennsylvania public school personnel perceptions of staff development practices and beliefs with a view to identifying some critical problems or needs.* Doctoral dissertation, The Pennsylvania State University.

Tough, A.M. (1967). *Learning without teachers.* Toronto, ON: Ontario Institute for the Study of Education.

Whitall, J., & Wood, F. (1979). Taking the threat out of classroom observation and feedback. *Journal of Teacher Education, 30,* 55-58.

Wood, F., Caldwell, S.D., & Cannon, A. (1984). *Report on staff development in the Fort Worth independent school district*. Fort Worth, TX: Fort Worth Independent School District.

Wood, F., Caldwell, S.D., & Thompson, S. (1986, Spring). Practical realities for school-based staff development. *Journal of Staff Development, 7*, 52-66.

Wood, F., Freeland, R., & Szabo, J. (1985, March). School improvement is more than school improvement. *Educational Leadership, 42*, 63-67.

Wood, F., Johnson, G., & Paden, J. (1984, March). Will this new round of recommendations for high schools make a difference? *Educational Leadership, 42*, 68-72.

Wood, F., & Neil, J. (1976). *A study of the effects of the /I/D/E/A/ clinical workshop: Report II*. Dayton, OH: Charles F. Kittering Foundation.

Wood, F., & Thompson, S. (1985). *Report on staff development in the St. Paul independent school district*. St. Paul, MN: Author.

Wood, F., Thompson, S., & Russell, F. (1981). Designing effective staff development programs. In B. Dillon-Peterson (Ed.), *Staff Development/Organizational Development*. Alexandria, VA: Association for Supervision and Curriculum Development.

Wood, F., & Thompson, S. (1981, Feb.). Guidelines for better staff development. *Educational Leadership, 37*, 374-378.

Zagarmi, P. (1981). Leadership and school climate: A data-based approach to administrative training. *Journal of Staff Development, 2*, 93-115.

Zagarmi, P., Betz, L., & Jensen, D. (1977, April). Teacher preferences in and perceptions of inservice. *Educational Leadership, 34*, 545-552.

The move to school-based improvement will require special inservice programs for boards of education, central office administrators, principals, teachers, and staff developers.

Chapter 3

Staff Development and the Individual

Successful staff development programs are based on knowledge about how individuals learn and develop.

Judy Arin-Krupp

Who has the ultimate responsibility for the development of an individual within an organization? Each individual must answer, "I do." Staff developers work hard to provide the best possible climate for learning, but individuals determine whether or not they will take advantage of opportunities for growth.

However, staff developers can maximize the chance that individuals will want to grow and change by planning learning activities based on knowledge about how adults learn and develop. This chapter focuses on those aspects of adult learning research that can be used practically by staff developers to plan and design learning activities. Discussion reflects the emphasis in research on how adults think about their learning and the importance of their level of self-direction and experience.

Meeting Needs of Adult Learners

Because individuals are complex, meeting individual needs can be a difficult job. Fortunately, adult learners share some common needs. All learners need a positive, growth-oriented environment in which to try new ideas. They also want practical and relevant new ideas oriented to their personal concerns.

Focus on Growth

Traditionally, staff development has focused on defects. The assumption was that teachers had something wrong with them that inservice training would correct (Krupp, 1986; Wood & Thompson, 1980). Research on adult learning and development mandates a switch to a growth orientation.

The fact that individuals need and desire lifelong learning is supported by studies of the internal hierarchy of needs (Maslow, 1971), of ego states (Loveinger, 1976), and of leisure-time choices and career changes for personal growth (Uris & Tarrant, 1983). Effective staff developers can help central-office administrators and principals create a norm for growth within a school or district.

Serve as models for growth. Openly discuss your own efforts to learn new knowledge and develop new skills. Ask to try out your skills in teachers' classrooms, during meetings, or wherever appropriate. Invite feedback and use it.

Reward growth. Establish a process to recognize and encourage those who demonstrate enthusiasm and the ability to integrate new ideas. Recognition can be provided through district or PTA newsletters, formal Teacher of the Month or Distinguished Teacher programs, invitations to give presentations to the board of education, articles in local newspapers, or before-school coffees.

Expect and accept failures. As people try using new skills, they usually get worse before they get better. Their smooth, expert performance becomes choppy and un-organized. Clearly discuss your expectations for "failures" of this kind as a necessary step toward growth. And remember that not all educational innovations should be "doomed to success." If a new curriculum, teaching strategy, or set of materials isn't as effective as you'd hoped, be prepared to revise or abandon it.

Make It Relevant and Practical

Individuals learn and apply learning activities that they perceive as both relevant and practical. Staff developers can emphasize these characteristics with a variety of strategies.

* **Use both personal and professional knowledge about participants in planning.** What are their out-of-school interests? What are their personal and professional goals?

* **Involve the learners in planning.** Ask learners for ideas and use as many of these as possible. Show respect for individuals who contributed unaccepted advice by taking time to let them know why their ideas did not become part of the program.

* **Use evaluation information to reassess needs.** Constantly monitor what the individual has learned, integrated, and acted upon to determine the next most meaningful step in the learning process.
* **Help participants tie their individual needs to school and district goals.** As Wood discussed in the preceding chapter, an organizational context that supports individual growth is provided when faculty members collaborate to determine goals and the staff development activities necessary to meet them.

Focus on Individual Interests and Needs

Provide opportunities for individual "entrepreneurs" to pursue their own growth, either alone or with a colleague or small group.

Encourage participants to write a proposal for their own staff development to meet an immediate need. The Brookfield (CT) school district allows staff members to formulate an Individualized Professional Development Plan (IPDP). The purpose of the IPDP is "to provide effective staff development opportunities to any Brookfield staff member who has a special or unique educational need or interest that requires time, funding, or consultation to develop" (Brookfield Public Schools, 1985). The Leadership Institute for Educators (LIFE) sponsored by the Northern Colorado BOCES (1987) in Longmont (CO) is another example. This program for administrators requires each to determine both a personal and a professional goal, suggest activities and persons to assist in accomplishing the goals, and determine a way to assess goal achievement. Connecticut's Summer Principals' Academy pairs principals from different districts to serve as advisors and peer coaches who help each other meet their personally chosen goals.

Traditionally, staff development has focused on defects. Research on adult learning and development mandates a switch to a growth orientation.

Establish (or develop contacts with) a Teachers' Center. Teachers' Centers respond to individual needs with activities such as workshops and minigrants focused on solving individual problems. Centers also provide an environment conducive to individualized learning where staff members can work on a project of their choosing or talk with peers.

Focus on Concerns

Relevant staff development should address the current concerns of the learner. The Concerns-Based Adoption Model (CBAM) evolved from studies of the concerns of teachers in new situations (Fuller at al., 1974; Hall & Rutherford, 1976). The stages of concern move from self, to task, to impact as experience with the change increases. Self-concerns include awareness, gaining information, and then wondering, "How will it affect me?" Task issues relate to management of the innovation. Impact concerns begin with questions about consequence, move to an interest in collaboration with others involved in the innovation, and then to an interest in refocusing or integrating the ideas with one's own creativity.

Each level of concern brings a level of use. Those at the self level of concern have not "bought in." They represent the nonusers. Those who are willing use the innovation first at a mechanical (management) level and work their way up to an integration (collaboration) level, and finally, to renewal where users seek new alternatives to established methodologies (Hall & Loucks, 1978; Hall et al., 1975).

The CBAM findings have practical implications for staff development programs. For example, in the early stages of an innovation, spend staff development time helping learners unfamiliar with an innovation understand the change and its effect on them. For those just beginning to use the innovation, staff development programs can address management concerns: organization, time, materials, and other resources. For personnel experienced with the innovation productive time can be spent sharing implementation strategies with others and discussing how certain modifications have proved successful (see Chapter 8).

Link to Resources

No single staff development program can meet all the needs of each learner. Assuring that learners attain their goals requires a system for linking individuals with available resources. Mentoring and networking both create such connections.

Not all educational innovations should be "doomed to success." If a new curriculum, teaching strategy, or set of materials isn't as effective as you'd hoped, be prepared to revise or abandon it.

Mentoring. Supporting the growth and development of another individual helps both the protege and the mentor. While gains for proteges are personal and situation-specific, mentors generally gain not only a sense of personal worth through feelings that others respect their experience, but they also make friends (Krupp, 1984; Rawlins & Rawlins, 1983). Proteges choose life mentors because they feel the individual has something to offer them. Many staff development programs have established mentor-teacher programs that link new employees with master teachers. These programs provide opportunities for peer-pal or apprenticeship training but rarely become life mentoring relationships. (See Chapter 5 for more on mentoring.)

Networking. Staff developers can help individuals contact other individuals or agencies that have specialized resources and can provide specific assistance. An individual might become a member of round-table study group, seminar, or support group. (See Metzdorf's description of the staff developer as linker in Chapter 1.)

Approaches to Learning

Styles and approaches to learning vary with the number of learners. Learners change in their style and approach as situations change. Those planning learning activities need to be sensitive to these variations.

Self-Directed or Other-Directed Learning

Adults vary in the amount of structure and direction they need to learn. Some learners require a high degree of direction in some parts of their learning and less direction in other aspects. Resentment builds when learners receive direction in areas where they feel self-motivated. On the other hand, people flounder and feel frustrated when told to use their own devices when they feel unsure.

Self-directed learners have the motivation to learn and the prerequisite skills both to accomplish the learning and to choose the means by which to learn. The self-directed learner appreciates a staff developer who offers support time, materials, and links to other resources.

Help participants tie their individual needs to school and district goals.

Other-directed learners may lack motivation, required skills for learning, or knowledge of how to accomplish the goal. As a result, other-directed learners achieve higher success levels when told the objectives and the processes required. Staff developers need to use flexible approaches, depending on the degree of self-direction the individual exhibits.

Individual Learning Styles

Each individual has an innate learning style that is modified with experience (Dunn & Dunn, 1978; Gregorc, 1979; Keirsey & Bates, 1984; Kolb, 1984; Smith & Bentley, 1975). Regardless of the research base, the same message emerges: People differ in how they learn. Each learning group most likely contains representatives of all learning styles and approaches. Staff developers can accommodate differences in several ways.

Vary techniques used to sequence and present content. Take into account such discrepant preferences as using breaks for eating non-sweet snacks, stretching, or smoking; the desire for group work or lecture; visual, kinesthetic, or auditory learning aids; and the possible need for an outline handed out in advance.

Frankly discuss differences in learning style. For example, when asking group members to introduce themselves, think about those who may feel they didn't come to hear other group members talk, they came to hear the presenter. Openly commenting on their feelings and legitimizing them as normal defuses frustration and anger. Similarly, talking about how individuals with different learning styles view things as diverse as authority figures, long reading assignments, rooms without windows, or risk-taking can help individuals accept those potential stumbling blocks to learning and still feel respected for their views. For example, some accept a leader because he or she has legitimate authority; others seek charisma; those with still another learning style want to know the leader's degrees and qualifications; and people with a fourth style only respect an individual figure who is good at verbal sparring. Knowledge of those differences helps participants and leaders understand individuals who constantly question, who hand in either extremely positive or negative evaluations of the same workshop, and who blindly accept statements made by the leader contrasted with those who seek out colorful and personal examples. Conflicts interfere less with learning when learners and leaders understand that learning style differences cause such discrepancies.

Developmental Stages and Life Experiences

Past experience creates a base for present learning. Each aspect of adult learners' previous experience and present life influences them during the learning process. Staff developers must view adult learners holistically and consider the developmental aspects that affect them during learning.

Assuring that learners attain their goals requires a system for linking individuals with available resources.

The developmental tasks of each life stage result in specific learning needs and desires. The same person at different ages has discrepant needs as he or she grows and changes. Individuals in their 20s often determine their career direction and, therefore, seek information on careers and validation for their own competence. Individuals turning 30 come face-to-face with career and identity decisions. Those in their 40s often find themselves in positions of authority and express a desire to improve their leadership skills. Individuals in their 50s have generally settled into their careers and appreciate opportunities to give to others. Linking developmental tasks and staff development activities maximizes learning for adults in each age group.

The following is meant to be descriptive, not prescriptive. All adults do not experience each age in a prescribed manner because each person brings to each stage his or her own individuality and past experience. Yet humans are amazingly similar and, therefore, many of the descriptions will fit for most adults.

The 20s

Because people in their 20s have never before experienced adulthood, they may feel unsure of themselves as they orient their lives around a career and/or a family. To use CBAM language, they express concern with self and task, and they ask two questions: "Can I?" and "How do I?" When possible they turn to more experienced persons to learn the "shoulds" and "oughts" of the job. Many of these young adults gradually develop a dream of what they will attain, how much they will earn, or a special project they will accomplish to prove that they have made it as an adult. The dream motivates the young person onward through degrees, job changes, babies, divorces, apartments, homes, major purchases, and mistakes. Young adults seek mentors to help them fulfill their dreams. Men emphasize responsibility in their quest for dream achievement, and women speak of self-awareness (Krupp, 1980; Krupp, 1981; Levinson et. al., 1978; Roberts & Newton, 1987).

Staff developers have used this information in the following ways to motivate young people to higher levels of productivity, enthusiasm, and learning.

Help with the "how to". Provide practical programs, such as how to create good bulletin boards, how to use a computer to assist instruction and keep records, how to conduct a parent-teacher conference, and how to handle the recalcitrant student.

Build confidence. To help the young adult build confidence and respond positively to the "Can I?" query, institute a support system for new and young faculty members. Mentor-induction programs that match master teachers with new teachers meet the needs of the new person as well as the more experienced one.

Share self-doubts. Staff developers who remember and talk about the fears and concerns they felt when they started to teach model "transparency" (Jourard, 1971). They let young adults "see into them." By doing so, they create a norm for sharing self-doubts. Such a norm helps bring concerns out into the open and permits the staff developer to intervene in a helpful way. It also prevents the blow-up that can result from keeping these doubts inside.

Learners require a high degree of direction in some parts of their learning and less direction in other aspects.

Identify real needs. Listen to and try to understand the young person in order to assure that suggested "shoulds" and "oughts" truly meet the needs of the individual. Those who follow this tack find they can influence the young adult over a long period of time. Those who ignore individual needs often suggest things the 20s person does not find helpful. As a result, the young adult no longer seeks support from that particular experienced individual.

The 30s

Individuation, the process by which people determine how they fit within the world (Jung, 1971), often initiates the transition to the 30s. People in their early 30s question their career, marriage, parenting, and geographic location. Men focus on concerns related to career, while women question many aspects of their existence (Bardwick, 1980; Bernard, 1981; Erikson, 1955; Harris et. al., 1986; Krupp, 1980; Levinson et al., 1978; Reinke et. al., 1985; Stewart, 1977). Change and inner turmoil characterize this transition.

Career-oriented people push hard for advancement during their 30s. Seeking advancement requires affirmation from others; this can cause feelings of insecurity or ambiguity about what will receive acclaim. Consequently, career-oriented individuals look for stability in other areas of their lives (Gould, 1978; Levinson et. al., 1978).

Many women expand their options during their 30s, integrating new activities and identities into their lives (Bardwick, 1980; Bernard, 1981; Harris et. al., 1986; Reinke et. al., 1985). Some retire from teaching to raise a family; others return to education or to the classroom.

By the end of their 30s, many become senior members of their occupational group. Other people ask their opinions. Now that they have achieved some degree of success, they may question the value of that achievement (Gould, 1978; Levinson et. al., 1978). Women who have long questioned their identity often begin to feel good about themselves. A woman in her 30s typically becomes her own person (Bardwick, 1980; Scarf, 1980; Stewart, 1977). Staff developers have directed professional development activities to meet some concerns of adults in their 30s in the following ways.

Help with personal concerns. Staff members experiencing the inner turmoil of the early years of the 30s may find their work affected. An employee assistance program (EAP) that is part of the staff development effort decreases absenteeism and increases productivity among school employees (Krupp, 1986). EAPs offer career counseling as well as counseling for substance abuse, family problems, and personal problems.

Aid with career stability and direction. Staff developers need to do all they can to reinforce and retain good personnel. Minigrants, visitations, money for national con-

Conflicts interfere less with learning when learners and leaders understand that learning style differences cause discrepancies.

ferences, and time to pursue a pet project related to the job are examples of staff development programs that emphasize individual strengths and reinforce staff members for staying on the job.

Recognize individual successes. Provide opportunities for teachers to share their ideas with others. For example, hold an annual teaching fair where teachers can exhibit novel methods or equipment. Invite teachers and administrators to offer workshops for their colleagues during staff development release time, faculty meetings, and before and after school. Provide opportunities for teachers to visit colleagues in other grades and schools.

Assist those who need/desire a career change. At this age, questions about career direction provide the opportunity to counsel those with marginal competency levels to leave education. Staff developers and administrators can offer all possible help for relocation (i.e., resume preparation, time off for interviews, and identification of available jobs).

The 40s

During the 40s, adults begin to view life as "time left to live" rather than an "endless expanse of possibilities," and neglected parts of the self seek fulfillment. Men, who usually emphasize assertiveness during the first half of life, tend to become more nurturing. Women, who often play nurturing roles from ages 20 to 40, frequently express their assertive selves. Similarly, those who had emphasized career now find it less central, while individuals new to a career delight in the job.

Some people feel disillusioned by their career gains; others feel tied to the job because of factors such as money invested in retirement, geographic inflexibility, or lack of desire to take a risk. Midlifers who lack career centrality and feel shackled to the job often become on-the-job retirees (Uris & Tarrant, 1983). They work from 8 to 3, but feel life starts after the work day. They lack a sense of direction and involvement on the job (Krupp, 1981; Krupp, 1986; Levinson et al., 1978; McGuigan, 1980; Scobey, 1984; Vaillant, 1977). During the 40s, people often find opportunities abound for linking personal developmental needs with school-related goals.

Meet differing needs of the sexes. Men often want to nurture during the second half of life when no one remains at home to nurture. Look for opportunities for males to nurture within the school. For example, a junior high school administrator in Michigan linked paired students with the worst discipline problems to their favorite teachers, males for the most part. The result: Student discipline problems lessened; teacher involvement and enthusiasm increased. Guidance teachers in a Minnesota high school complained about their case loads. The administrators paired students needing guidance, but not counseling, with a teacher with whom they worked once a month on writing applications for jobs or college and learning how to act during an interview and how to dress for success. Students felt they got more attention, the teachers' absenteeism diminished, and their enthusiasm and interest in the students increased (Krupp, 1986).

Women, who become more assertive, say what they want, fight for students' rights, start new programs, and get what they need to do the job effectively. Their forcefulness and enthusiasm bring excitement into the school. They openly seek new learning and willingly try new interventions. Invite them to take on leadership roles as chairs for faculty or curriculum committees. Encourage them to seek additional responsibilities in their school, such as developing a new program of after-school activities for students. Involve them in outreach into the community.

Capitalize on outside interests. Those who feel less career centrality, experience disillusionment, simulate retirement on the job, or spend more time on outside interests respond positively when leaders bring their outside interests into their professional lives. For example, the Simsbury, Conn., school district offers a full-day staff development program that includes not only workshops but also a display of employees' arts and crafts, musical accompaniment by workers, and a chance for staff members to teach their avocations. Many middle schools have "fired-up" burned out staff members with the institution of an activity period when teachers teach minicourses to students in the teachers' areas of special interest.

In a Massachusetts program, a staff developer asked an on-the-job retiree to videotape a staff development session so that those unable to attend could view it later. He agreed. One thing led to another, and he now runs a video studio in the high school. He comes in earlier, stays later, and has a cadre of children who work with him.

Develop leadership. Use people for whom career has achieved greater centrality. Ask these people to give workshops, to chair or participate on curriculum committees, to develop new interdisciplinary programs, to take children on a camping trip, or to represent the faculty at a parent-teacher meeting or conference.

The 50s

In the 50s, adults become "keepers of the meaning." They know their own values and want them maintained by society. They can respond rigidly when challenged (Vaillant & Milofsky, 1980).

At the same time, many adults "mellow" in their 50s. They feel the "die is cast." They ask, "Is it worth getting upset?" They take a more relaxed approach to life and its problems (Bardwick, 1980; Harris et. al., 1986; Levinson et. al., 1978; Reinke et. al., 1985).

Retirement concerns those in their 50s. They wonder whether they will have enough money to maintain their life style. They want significant activities to keep them busy and make them feel worthwhile. They want to know when and how to retire (Dreyfack, 1980).

Listen and acknowledge. Listening motivates. Experienced adults who know their values and goals want to share their past with others. They feel respected and esteemed when others seek their opinions. (Krupp, 1986). The best professional development effort may not succeed if the staff developer does not seek, listen to, and acknowledge the past experience of the older employee.

Capitalize on experience. The mellow employee can either provide a stable sense of continuity to others or can become non-caring. Staff developers can involve the mature person in mentor-teacher programs, on staff development committees, and in special projects to build parent and community support.

The non-caring person presents a staff development challenge. Ask the question, "What key will unlock the door to that person's creativity?" For one person, the door opens when the staff developer provides resources and encouragement to try a pet project. For another, creativity may emerge when the person has time to help a disadvantaged youngster.

Figure 3.1
Assessing Your Program

1. Are you familiar with and is your staff development program based on the basic concepts of adult learning and development?
2. Do your district, school, and staff development programs promote continuous, lifelong growth?
3. Does your staff development program allow time for staff developers to improve their listening skills and to use those skills to learn about workers?
4. Does your staff development program take into account
   * The learner's past experience
   * The links between the needs of the learner, the school, and the district
   * Varied approaches and choices
   * The desires of learners and their stages of development - their wants and needs
   * Continuous needs assessment and use of program evaluation data to plan future learning activities for individuals

---

Figure 3.2
Competencies

1. Possess flexibility in leadership style as the learner's level of self-directedness, learning style, and concerns warrants.
2. Know individual participants in a staff development program in terms of interests, strengths, concerns, and out-of-reach demands.
3. Use program evaluation feedback as needs reassessment.
4. Have a thorough knowledge of available resources (e.g., teacher centers, universities, agencies) and develop appropriate linkage with staff members.
5. Involve individuals in planning.
6. Encourage networking and mentoring.
7. Model lifelong learning and growth.
8. Know how age, stage, and orientation to growth and learning affect attitudes toward staff development.
9. Use a variety of techniques and formats as individual learner need demands.

Address retirement concerns. Provide workshops that address retirement concerns such as financial planning and the pros and cons of early retirement. Those with a diverse identity have the highest sense of self upon retirement and worry less before they retire (Dreyfack, 1980). Help individuals to feel worthwhile in areas other than those they teach by integrating their interests into extracurricular activities or courses.

Conclusion

This overview of adult learning and development represents only the tip of the iceberg. Participants will negate the best staff development unless staff developers consider individual needs, learning approaches, and developmental needs of the learners. Working with adults may produce stress because adults define their own ideas of excellence. Knowing yourself and others minimizes that stress, maximizes effectiveness, and makes both the staff developer and the staff member more productive and more professional.

References

Bardwick, J.M. (1980). The seasons of a woman's life. In D. McGuigan (Ed.), *Women's lives: New theory, research and policy*. Ann Arbor, MI: University of Michigan Center of Continuing Education of Women.

Bernard, J. (1981). *The female world*. New York: The Free Press.

Brookfield Public Schools. (1985). *Guidelines: Individual professional development plan*. Available from staff development office, Brookfield Public Schools, Brookfield, CT 06804

Dreyfack, R. (1980). *What an executive should know about successful retirement in a changing economy*. Chicago: The Dartnell Corporation.

Dunn, R., & Dunn, K. (1978). *Teaching students through their individual learning styles: A practical approach*. Reston, VA: Reston Publishing Company.

Erikson, E.H. (1955). *Childhood and society.* New York: W.W. Norton and Co.

Fuller, F.F., Parsons, J., & Watkins. (1974). *Concerns of teachers: Research and reconceptualization.* Austin, TX: Research and Development Center for Teacher Education, University of Texas. (ERIC Document Reproduction Service NO. 091 439).

Gould, R. (1978). *Transformations: Growth and change in adult life.* New York: Simon and Schuster.

Gregorc, A. (1979). Learning/teaching styles: Their nature and effects. In *Student learning styles: Diagnosing and prescribing programs.* Reston, VA: National Association of Secondary School Principals.

Hall, G.E., & Loucks, S.F. (1978, September). Teacher concerns and a basis for facilitating and personalizing staff development. *Teachers College Record, 80*(1), 36-53.

Hall, G.E., Loucks, S.F., Rutherford, W.L., & Newlove, B.W. (1975, Spring). Level of use of the innovation: A framework for analyzing innovation adoption. *Journal of Teacher Education, 26,* 52-56.

Hall, G.E. & Rutherford, W.L. (1976). Concerns of teachers about implementing team teaching. *Educational Leadership, 34,* 227-234.

Harris, R.L., Ellicott, A.M., & Holmes, D.S. (1986, August). The timing of psychsocial transitions and changes in women's lives: An examination of women aged 45-60. *Journal of Personality and Social Psychology, 51*(2), 409-416.

Jourard, S.M. (1971). *The transparent self.* New York: D. Van Norstrand Company.

Jung, C. (1971). The stages of life. In J. Campbell (Ed.), *The portable Jung.* New York: Viking Press.

Keirsey, D., & Bates, M. (1984). *Please understand me: Character and temperament types.* Del Mar, CA: Prometheus Nemesis Book Company.

Kolb, D. (1984). *Experiential learning: Experience as the source of learning and development.* New Jersey: Prentice-Hall, Inc.

Krupp, J.A. (1980). *A phenomenological study of teacher perceptions of life developmental changes as related to inservice behaviors and needs.* Unpublished doctoral dissertation, University of Connecticut, Storrs, Conn.

Krupp, J.A. (1981). *Adult development: Implications for staff development.* Colchester, CT: Project RISE. Available from Adult Development and Learning, 40 McDivitt Drive, Manchester, CT 06040.

Krupp, J.A. (1984). *Mentor and protege perceptions of mentoring relationships in an elementary and secondary school in Connecticut.* Paper presented at the meeting of American Educational Research Association, New Orleans, LA.

Krupp, J.A. (Fall, 1986). Using the power of the principalship to motivate experienced teachers. *The Journal of Staff Development, 7,* 100-111.

Krupp, J.A. (Spring, 1986). Staff development: Problems that reveal solutions. *Insights into Professional Development,* Hartford, CT: Connecticut Organization for Professional Development.

Levinson, D.J., Darrow, C., Klein, E., Levinson, M., & McKee, B. (1978). *The seasons of a man's life.* New York: Alfred A. Knopf.

Loevinger, J. (1976). *Ego development: Conceptions and theories.* San Francisco, CA: Jossey-Bass.

Maslow, A. (1971). *The farther reaches of human nature.* New York: Viking Press.

McGuigan, D.G. (Ed.). (1980). *Women's lives: New theory, research and policy.* Ann Harbor, MI: University of Michigan Center for Continuing Education of Women.

Northern Colorado BOCES (1987). *L.I.F.E.* Available from NCBOCES, 830 S. Lincoln, Longmont, CO 80501

Rawlins, M.E., & Rawlins, L. (1983, October). Mentoring and networking for helping professionals. *The Personnel and Guidance Journal, 62,* 116-118.

Reinke, B.J., Holmes, D.S., & Harris, R.L. (1985, May). The timing of psychosocial changes in women's lives: The years 25-45. *Journal of Personality and Social Psychology, 48,* 1353-1364.

Roberts, P., & Newton, P. (1987, June). Levinsonian studies of women's adult development. *Psychology and Aging, 2,* 154-163.

Scarf, J. (1980). *Unfinished business: Pressure points in the lives of women.* New York: Doubleday and Co., Inc.

Scobey, J. (1984). *I'm a stranger here myself.* New York: St. Martin's/Marek.

Smith, P.B., & Bentley. (1975). *Data bank guide to learning styles: TIP mainstreaming mildly handicapped students into the regular classroom.* Austin, TX: Education Service Center.

Stewart, W. (1977). *A psychological study of the formation of the early adult life structure in women.* Unpublished doctoral dissertation, Columbia University, NY.

Uris, A., & Tarrant, J.J. (1983). *Career stages: Surmounting the crises of working life.* New York: Seaview/Putnam.

Vaillant, G.E. (1977). *Adaptation to life.* Boston: Little, Brown and Company.

Vaillant, G.E., & Milofsky, E. (1980, Nov.). Natural history of male psychological health: IX Empirical evidence for Erikson's model of the life cycle. *American Journal of Psychiatry, 137*(ll), 1348-1359.

Wood, F.H., & Thompson, S. (1981). Guidelines for better staff development. *Educational Leadership, 37,* 374-378.

View adult learners holistically and consider the developmental aspects that affect them during learning.

Chapter 4

Putting It All Together: An Integrated Staff Development Program

A comprehensive staff development program will enable a school district to identify and respond to district, school, and individual needs — with minimal duplication of effort or waste of resources.

Susan Ellis

The preceding chapters have described the elements of effective district-based staff development programs, school-based improvement efforts, and individual adult learning. Although Metzdorf, Wood, and Krupp address different components of staff development programs, each assumes that htose components are embedded in a comprehensive program embracing district, school, and individual goals and needs. As Wood pointed out, although many researchers and practitioners advocate focusing on the school as the unit of change, they also know that school-based change is most likely to occur when the principles of adult development and learning are incorporated into the design of that change and when the school's goals are supported by district-level resources. In addition, some needs are truly districtwide; responding to them effectively requires improvement efforts in all schools.

This chapter describes the processes and procedures of a comprehensive staff development program that enable a school district to identify and respond to district, school, and individual needs with minimal duplication of effort or waste of resources. To cover all important elements, this chapter is written as if a district were starting from scratch to build a staff development program although, as Metzdorf made clear, that is rarely the case. Questions to guide assessing your program are outlined in Figure 4.1.

Philosophy

The first step in creating a comprehensive program is developing a district philosophy of staff development. The purpose is to spell out the beliefs that will guide the creation of the program structure and to secure support from those who will provide the program (taxpayers), from those who will engage in it (district staff), and from those who will be its ultimate beneficiaries (students, their parents, and the community at large).

Consequently, representatives of all interested groups should be involved in this process, including teachers, administrators, aides, the board of education, the teachers' bargaining unit, secretaries, maintenance personnel, parents, students, and community members. Because most participants may be newcomers to the principles of adult learning and staff development as well as the process of change and organizational development, the facilitator for this process should be able to assess the needs of the group and provide necessary information and training.

Goal Setting

Once a philosophy has been developed and agreed upon, the mechanisms for putting that philosophy into practice can be created. The first of these mechanisms is goal setting. A comprehensive staff development program is based on goals at the district, school, and individual levels. Goals provide focus for staff development efforts as well as a way to evaluate their success.

District Goals

The board of education is responsible for setting long-term, district-level improvement goals based on current needs assessments (e.g., student reading scores compared with student ability measures) as well as projected needs (e.g., the demands of an information age on its citizens). In addition, the board must weigh competing demands for improvement and choose the district's priorities.

The superintendent is responsible for providing sufficient information about the state of the school system so the board can make informed decisions about district goals. This information should be generated from a variety of sources: cyclical evaluations of each program area (staggered so that everything is not under review at the same time); regular examination of each school's functioning; continual search of the educational literature for new, effective practices; and ongoing dialogue with business and community leaders to determine skills that students are likely to need to succeed as adults.

Responsibility for generating this information should be spread throughout the district and involve all teachers and administrators or their representatives. Districtwide curriculum committees can propose to a coordinator, director, or assistant superintendent goals based on either evaluation of student performance in their area or new research-based methods of instruction. Central office administrators are most likely to be given responsibility for seeking information from education research and from the community, but teachers or

Figure 4.1
Assessing Your Program

1. **Does our district have a written philosophy of staff development?**
   A. Was the statement of philosophy created jointly by representatives of the school board, administrators, teachers, teachers' bargaining unit, secretaries, maintenance personnel, parents, and students?
   B. Is the statement of philosophy readily available? Is it supported by staff members, parents, and community members?

2. **Does our district have long term, district level improvement goals?**
   A. Are the goals based on current needs assessment or projections of future needs?
   B. Have appropriate administrators, working with committees, developed action plans to implement these goals?
   C. Are sufficient funds budgeted for the activities necessary to accomplish the goals?
   D. Is time provided for planning, curriculum writing, training, and evaluation?

3. **Does each school in our district have school-based improvement goals?**
   A. Were these goals developed by a committee representing administration, teachers, parents, and perhaps students?
   B. Have teachers who will be involved in implementing these goals written appropriate action plans?
   C. Have sufficient funds been budgeted at the building level for the activities that are named in the action plans?
   D. Is time provided for planning, training, peer coaching, evaluation, and other improvement activities?

4. **Does each staff member in our district have personal goals for professional improvement?**
   A. Has each individual written an action plan for implementing those goals?
   B. Does the district sponsor staff development activities to support individual goals?
   C. Are financial support and release time available for additional staff development activities that will enable staff members to accomplish their individual goals?

5. **Is one individual responsible for overseeing all aspects of the staff development program?**
   A. Is that individual clearly identified by title?
   B. Is that individual given sufficient time and resources to provide the coordination and service needed at all levels of the program?
   C. Does that individual possess the competencies to provide the coordination and service needed at all levels of the program?

6. **Does the district have a districtwide staff development committee comprising teachers, administrators, clerical and maintenance staff, and perhaps parents, board of education members, and community members?**
   A. Does that committee frequently examine the structure, policies, and procedures of the staff development program and adjust them whenever appropriate?
   B. Do those committee members serve as active liaisons between the district level staff developer and their various constituencies?

administrators can also be part of that process by sharing information learned at educational conferences and out-of-district workshops. Moreover, principals can contribute information about their schools that may have districtwide implications.

Once the board of education has weighed proposals by the superintendent and has chosen district goals for the next three to five years, the superintendent or other central office administrators decide which administrators will be responsible for developing action plans for each goal. Action plans should specify objectives, activities, personnel, target completion dates, check points, and methods of evaluation to be used. They should also include a space for evaluation data when the objective is met (Figure 4.2). Some goals may fall under the aegis of one individual. For example, developing and piloting a new health curriculum for 8th grade students might be given to a coordinator of science or a teacher leader for health. Other goals will involve the efforts of several people. For example, improving reading comprehension in the content areas could be the responsibility of all curriculum coordinators or teacher leaders.

Writing district-level action plans should involve the people who will carry them out. To continue with the examples used above, the teacher leader for health might bring together a group of science teachers, guidance counselors, and psychologists to develop a plan for writing and piloting a new health curriculum. Subject area coordinators might create a committee of teachers representing several disciplines to develop a plan for improving reading comprehension.

Figure 4.2
Plan of Action

Plan of Action

Objective or Priority:

Action Steps	Completion Indicators	Check Point Dates	Completion Date	Evaluation Criteria	Evaluation

When district-based goals require action in schools, school-based teams of teachers and an administrator need to develop action plans appropriate to their school's specific needs. In a small district, the central office administrator responsible for the goal may participate in this planning; in a large district, the administrator might simply review action plans from each school. Responsibility for implementation is thus shared by the principal and the central office administrator.

School Goals

Not all district goals will affect all schools. Effects will differ because goals are aimed at students on a particular level, such as improving the teaching of writing in the primary grades, or because a school has already accomplished or is not yet ready to work on a district goal. In addition, individual schools have problems not necessarily shared by others in the district. Problems can be as diverse as a large number of latchkey students, declining or low staff morale, a sudden influx of non-English-speaking students, a moribund creative dramatics program, or a high proportion of first-year teachers. Schools also have unique assets that can be tapped for improvement efforts. These might include staff members or parents with unusual talents, special locations that lend themselves to creative outdoor or cultural curriculums, or unique community resources that can be brought into the school.

A comprehensive staff development program is based on goals at the district, school, and individual levels. Goals provide focus for staff development efforts as well as a way to evaluate their success.

For these reasons, as well as those described in Chapter 2, each school in a district should have its own school improvement goals.

Wood advocates developing school goals through a committee consisting of teachers, the principal, community leaders, parents, and central office representatives. Many schools — especially secondary schools — also include students in this process. School districts that develop clear district goals and action plans may not need a central office representative on each school committee, if the principal participated in developing the district level goals and is knowledgeable about plans for implementing them. In such districts, a subcommittee of the board of education, as well as the superintendent or another central office administrator, might meet with each school committee after it has established its goals to learn why they were selected. Such district-school communication often leads the school board to consider adopting a new district-level goal — one that surfaced through the goal-setting process in several schools.

School goals need not duplicate district goals. For example, an elementary school might elect to focus its improvement efforts in two areas: math instruction and parent-school communication. Improving students' understanding of mathematical concepts might be a district goal on which the school decided to expend more effort than the district called for. Improving communication between parents and school could be that school's own concern and one not duplicated by other schools in the district.

Once school goals are chosen, committees representing those who will carry them out should be formed to write action plans. As noted above, if the school goal duplicates or supports a district goal, the action plan should be reviewed by the central office administrator responsible for the district goal. Action plans for goals pertaining to just one school should be reviewed by the central office administrator to whom the school's principal reports. Central office administrators can help develop plans, locate additional resources, eliminate duplication of efforts, and create links between schools that have similar goals.

Individual Goals

Providing for individual, as well as district and school goals, enables a school system to keep individual teachers and administrators excited about their work and to bring new ideas into the district. Individual goals allow for different learning styles and should respond to different experience and readiness levels. These goals should aim for the kind of individualized learning that most educators would like to see in classroom instruction.

As suggested in Chapter 3, individual goals are particularly appropriate for self-directed learners, but they can be adapted to the needs of other-directed learners as well. Whether or not individual goals are tied to evaluation or recertification, they can be shared — and even jointly developed — with an administrator who can provide suggestions and direction if

When district-based goals require action in schools, school-based teams of teachers and an administrator need to develop action plans appropriate to their school's specific needs.

needed. Administrators can also bring together staff members who have similar goals and can encourage them to write joint goals, thus fostering collegiality.

Individual goals may, but need not, tie to school or district goals. Teachers and administrators who welcome the freedom to develop personal goals are not negating or ignoring their responsibility to support and implement district and school goals. Instead, they are choosing to gain additional skills or knowledge that will provide personal satisfaction and increased professional competence.

Like district and school goals, individual goals should be translated into action plans. If accomplishing these goals is part of the formal evaluation process, the staff member's evaluator will review the action plan. To encourage risk taking and experimentation among staff members, many districts separate individual staff development goals from evaluation for tenure or promotion. In such districts, teachers may develop their own action plans with no administrative review. Administrators, however, are generally expected to share their personal goals and action plans with their supervisors.

Resource Allocation

No staff development program will succeed without enough money to buy the time and resources necessary to develop, carry out, and evaluate improvement plans. The National Staff Development Council suggests a minimum of 1 percent of the district's operating budget. But availability is just as important as the amount of money allocated. A district with a comprehensive staff development program will put its money behind its commitment — in each curriculum area undergoing improvement and in each school. Funds for supporting individual goals should also be clearly identified.

District Level Resources

Every time a board of education adopts an improvement goal, it must budget for several years appropriate funds for the program to be improved. These funds should cover the projected span of the program and costs of needs assessment, planning, piloting, implementation, and maintenance. Funding plans should include specific line items for release time or compensation for staff work, consultant fees, travel, materials, equipment, and supplemental clerical help. The budget may need to be adjusted as action plans are written and each phase is carried out. If resources diminish, the plans may have to be abridged. Control of the day-to-day use of improvement money rests with the administrator charged with effecting the improvement. That person is usually subject to review by a supervisor.

In addition to money earmarked for specific goals, discretionary funds may be budgeted to enable the program administrator to sponsor special projects, award minigrants, support

Providing for individual, as well as district and school goals, enables a school system to keep individual teachers and administrators excited about their work and to bring new ideas into the district.

staff attendance at national conferences, and otherwise create or respond to opportunities for staff members' continued growth.

School Resources

Schools need funds, controlled at the school level, to support their own improvement efforts. Districts may allocate an amount to each school based on its number of certified staff members, its number of pupils, or some other appropriate formula. Schools with special needs may receive additional funds. The specific line-item allocation of these funds should be decided by each school's staff development committee in response to the goals and action plans developed by that school.

A portion of school staff-development funds may also be set aside to support staff members' personal improvement goals. In that case, granting such funds is usually the responsibility of a school committee that follows procedures established at the district level to provide equity throughout the district.

In districts with decentralized budgeting, schools can also allocate funds for staff development that supports improvements in specific program areas such as social studies and language arts. The principal oversees expenditure of school staff development monies, subject to review by a supervisor. In the case of school-based curriculum funds, the curriculum supervisor may also oversee those funds.

Individual Resources

Different structures exist for providing funds to support individual staff development projects. As mentioned above, some school systems locate staff development funds both in individual schools and on a district level within program areas. Pupil personnel services such as guidance, special education, and school psychologists might also have their own funds.

A staff member should be able to apply for funds from either a school or a program area. Some districts also allocate funds to a central office staff development administrator who supports projects that fall outside particular programs. Other districts may have a single pot of staff development money earmarked for individual projects. Usually a districtwide committee reviews application for these funds using district criteria.

A very different mechanism for providing individual staff development is exemplified by a teachers' center. Although some centers, such as those in New York State, are state supported and others are run by teachers' unions, some are district supported. Teachers use the center on their own initiative. They may request and receive release time for center programs; funds for substitutes may be budgeted by the center, the schools, or the central office.

Optimal scheduling of release time for staff training is at regular intervals during the school year so that participants have time between sessions to try out their new learning and come back for problem-solving or more training.

The amount of financial support available to individual staff members depends in part on a district's resources. However, it is not necessary — and may not be wise — for the district to bear all costs of individual staff development. As the Rand study of federal innovations indicated, teachers who are paid to attend workshops may value them less than do teachers who pay to participate in the same programs. Receiving partial funding for attending a conference or taking a course enables staff members to attend the activity and feel supported by their districts. Requiring staff members to spend some of their own money may actually increase the effort expended and the value received.

Release Time

In addition to releasing staff members to work on projects, attend conferences and workshops, or visit other schools and programs, many districts also schedule release time for staff development activities. Staff development release can be full days, half days, early release afternoons, or a combination of these. Scheduling of release time is often influenced, or dictated, by state regulations about the minimum length of the school day and year. Release time is also influenced by contract stipulations about the length of the teacher's day and year, tradition ("We *never* come back before Labor Day!"), and parental or staff preferences. Some districts schedule one or two full days at the beginning or the end of the school year; however, these times are least likely to be productive for introducing new ideas or providing training. In late August or early September, most staff members are eager to get ready for the opening of school, not to work on improving their performance. Similarly, in late June, most staff members are tired from end-of-year procedures and are looking forward to getting away from school for a while, not to focusing their attention on what they will be doing differently the following year. (However, some find late June or late August good times for planning activities). Optimal scheduling of release time for staff training is at regular intervals during the school year so that participants have time between sessions to try out their new learning and come back for problem-solving or more training.

A district with a comprehensive program may designate portions of the scheduled release time for working on district goals, school goals, and individual goals. Participation in specific activities during district release time might be required of teachers. Whether participation in activities on individual school release time is voluntary or required is determined by the faculty committee planning the sessions. Participation in individual professional development activities is clearly at the discretion of the individual staff member. Requiring an individual to choose from among workshops — no matter how many are offered — does not foster self-directed learning. Allowing a self-designed option, like that described in Chapter 3, encourages staff members to take responsibility for their own learning and enables those with unique goals to undertake projects appropriate for them.

A very different mechanism for providing individual staff development is exemplified by a teachers' center.

Coordination of an Integrated Staff Development Program

Coordinating a staff development program that provides for district, school, and individual goal-setting and improvement can be accomplished in several ways. The most common structure includes a central office staff developer who is likely to be a staff person but may be an administrator. (Common administrative titles are assistant superintendent for curriculum, instruction, and staff development; assistant superintendent for personnel and staff development; and director of instruction and staff development. Common non-administrative titles are director, coordinator, or teacher leader for staff development.) If district staff developers are not administrators, they usually report to assistant superintendents.

Staff Developer

The role of the district-level staff developer varies with the size of the district but usually includes the following functions:

* Conducting needs assessments to determine the kinds of activities that will support individual professional development.
* Providing workshops and training programs to respond to individual needs as well as to implement any noncurricular district goals. (Most staff developers are effective trainers and also hire district and out-of-district trainers and consultants.)

* Training staff members to give workshops.
* Training a cadre of teacher trainers.
* Working with the district-level staff development committee to develop, monitor, and evaluate districtwide staff development policies and procedures.
* Training teacher members of the district-level staff development committee to be leaders of their schools' staff development efforts.
* Serving as a peer coach for staff members.
* Facilitating the staff development efforts of central office program leaders.
* Disseminating information about out-of-district training opportunities.
* Publishing the district guide to staff development.
* Publishing a staff development newsletter that highlights district, school-based, and individual staff development efforts as well as current research on effective practices.
* Serving as a resource — and finding other resources — for all district personnel engaged in staff development.

In large districts, staff developers may run a staff development academy or a teachers' center. They may have a staff of trainers supported by clerical help, an audiovisual department that makes training materials and videotapes training programs, and a printing department that produces training materials. In small districts, they may operate alone or

---

The district level staff development committee plays a crucial role in coordinating a comprehensive staff development program.

---

with the assistance of a part-time secretary.

The advantage of having nonadministrative staff developers is that they can serve as ombudsmen and resources to everyone in the district without raising concerns about their evaluative role. Staff developers can also — without violating confidences — be liaisons between teachers and principals, between school and central office administrators, among central office administrators, and between everyone and the superintendent.

District Level Staff Development Committee

The district level staff development committee, chaired by the district staff developer, contains one or more teacher representatives from every school — usually more from large schools — as well as representatives for the bargaining unit, building administrators, curriculum coordinators, and central office administrators. In some districts, parents and community members also participate. This committee plays a crucial role in coordinating a comprehensive staff development program. Participants bring the perspectives of the schools or roles they represent to the committee, and they communicate the committee's decisions to their constituencies. When changes in program structure, policy, or procedures seem warranted, this body deliberates for the entire school system. The district-level staff development committee also keeps the staff developer informed of problems, concerns, or successes throughout the system.

Central Office Administrators

The district staff developer reports to a central office administrator, usually to one assistant superintendent and occasionally to two, such as the assistant superintendents for elementary and secondary education. Administrators review all action plans from schools and programs and provide staff developers with information that will enable them to make appropriate linkages and to provide training to help administrators carry out their staff development responsibilities.

Figure 4.3
Competencies

The competencies are those needed by a district level staff developer. These people hold titles such as Coordinator of Staff Development, Professional Development Director, or Assistant Superintendent for Curriculum and Staff Development.

Knowledge (theory, research, good practice)
1. Adult development, adult learning.
2. Organizational development, staff development, and the change process.
3. Effective group process.
4. Effective schools and effective teaching practices.
5. Effective training designs.
6. Needs Assessment.
7. Evaluation.

Skills (A district-based staff developer must possess these skills or have the support of others who do.)
1. Diagnosing group members' needs.
2. Training participants in needed skills, which may include group process, goal setting, budgeting, writing action plans, writing curriculum, designing evaluation strategies, peer coaching, supervision.
3. Modeling effective skills, including those listed in 2.
4. Providing communication between and among participants at all levels of the district.
5. Monitoring staff development planning and implementation at all levels; providing assistance as needed.
6. Communicating staff development priorities to community members.
7. Evaluating the effectiveness of the district's staff development program.

Conclusion

This chapter has focused on the structure necessary for an integrated staff development program. Perhaps more important than any structure, however, is the feeling that pervades a district — the sense that all in school system are involved in continuous professional improvement. You know such districts when you visit or work in them. Teachers and administrators talk about teaching and learning, and students; they solve problems together;

and they expect to succeed in their efforts to improve their schools. This climate is not so much a result of a structure that provides staff development as of a commitment to a philosophy of staff development, a belief that we all are lifelong learners, and that working together we can learn to do almost anything.

Perhaps more important than any structure, however, is the feeling that pervades a district — the sense that all in the school system are involved in continuous professional improvement.

Chapter

5

Designs for Learning

If staff development activities are to respond to the diverse needs of participants, they must be multifaceted . . . representing an array of structures, designs, and processes that can be matched to particular learning outcomes.

Sarah L. Levine
and
Nancy E. Broude

Once the context for learning is established and the needs of the district, school, and individual determined, what will be the specific designs for learning? Designs for learning are structures and formats to achieve specific professional outcomes. They are "learning" designs because the goal of staff development is to teach new knowledge, skills, and attitudes.

If staff development activities are to respond to the diverse needs of participants, they must be multifaceted. Workshops, for example, may combine small-group work with lecture and demonstration; presentations may incorporate interactive exercises or visuals. Designs for learning can be relatively stable structures, like support groups, or dynamic processes, such as building a climate of readiness or implementing innovative practices. This chapter approaches learning designs from each of these perspectives, offering staff developers an array of structures, designs, and processes that can be matched to particular learning outcomes.

Assumptions About Staff Development

Designs for learning must incorporate basic assumptions about adult learning and effective staff development. Specifically, successful staff development:

* Reflects and incorporates the principles of adult learning and adult growth.
* Balances district, school, and individual needs.
* Fosters both increased independence and interdependence.
* Takes account of desired results.
* Requires a substantial amount of personal involvement, commitment to the program, participation, and time.

Establishing a Context for Growth

An essential element of successful staff development is, as Wood notes in Chapter 2, "a positive, healthy school climate that includes trust, open communication, and peer support for changes in practice." Engaging participants in the design of staff development activities helps ensure that their immediate learning needs are addressed. Building individual and group commitments to new programs or practices helps to initiate and sustain positive attitudes, active participation during the learning process, and willingness to change and maintain new behaviors. Both time and continuing practice are important components of learning and perfecting new skills, and must be part of the learning context.

Building a climate of readiness for learning skills, changing attitudes or adopting new behaviors cannot be underestimated. Time and energy spent on developing a receptive learning context is critical. Staff developers can monitor readiness through formal and informal assessments, such as a survey of needs or conversations with key participants. Helping faculty members get to know one another, supporting open communication, and assisting participants in developing and refining decision making and problem solving skills are all essential for successful staff development.

Matching Structures and Outcomes

Staff development activities can meet a range of outcomes from enhancing educational effectiveness to stimulating personal and professional learning and growth. More specifically, they can be targeted to several outcomes:

* Increased *awareness*
* Enhanced *knowledge*
* Modified *attitudes*
* Changed *behaviors*
* New, strengthened, or refined *skills*

* Established or changed *school climate or culture*
* Renewed individual or group *motivation*
* *Team building* and strengthened *collegiality*

Identifying intended outcomes is an early step in determining staff development designs. The next step is to match outcomes and designs. If initial staff development outcomes are awareness or motivation, presentation techniques such as lecture, film, or video, followed by questions and discussion, are useful first steps. Changing attitudes or behaviors requires more complex and extensive strategies, such as small-group workshops over time, demonstrations, practice, coaching, and feedback.

Designs for Learning

Lecture/Presentation

Often, the training design is the lecture or presentation. Although listening is the primary mode of learning for this design, staff developers can expand the possibilities for learning by including charts, overheads and other visuals; by allowing time for questions and discussion; and by varying format with a combination of designs (i.e., large-group presentation followed by small-group discussions for processing).

Lecture/presentation is effective for conveying information, raising awareness, and generating interest. When introducing new procedures that have little latitude for discretion, presentation with time for clarification and questions can be ideal. When new

---

Identifying intended outcomes is an early step in determining staff development designs.

---

procedures require more than explanation and clarification, demonstration and practice can be built into the design.

Panel presentations are a variation on the lecture/presentation method. Panels are particularly useful for exploring different points of view and including practitioners as presenters or respondents.

Workshop

Workshops typically provide small- to moderate-sized groups with structured activities including presentations focused on a given topic or skill. They often include active participation, such as role playing. To help teachers and administrators learn a new skill, for instance, a workshop leader might first make a brief presentation, then use a film to illustrate the skill in practice, then engage the participants through discussion and small-group work. If the skill being taught is, for instance, how to make use of diverse teaching styles, participants might be asked to plan and teach a lesson using an array of techniques. The workshop could conclude with a discussion and critique of what has been learned, suggestions for implementation, and recommendations for follow-up sessions.

Multiple workshops designed and delivered over time at the school level can be combined with supervised practice or peer coaching to ensure transfer and maintenance.

When skill acquisition and changed behavior are desired outcomes, complex training designs are required. Joyce and Showers (1982, 1983) recommend a five-step approach including presentation of materials, demonstration of skills, practice, coaching and feedback.

Support Groups

All successful staff development practices include support as a central component, and in recent years, various kinds of support groups have surfaced as effective contexts for adult learning. In *collegial support groups* and *quality circles* small groups of educators work together on shared problems and practices. While the organization and focus of a group may be idiosyncratic, most share a number of key conditions for learning. Participation is voluntary. Together with staff development facilitators, group members determine the focus of discussion and problem solving. Sharing and shared or reciprocal status are the norms. Each group member or partner has the opportunity and responsibility to give and receive support and feedback.

Collegial support groups help reduce isolation and improve communication, team building, collegiality, instruction, and personal and professional esteem. Feedback is formative. Participants gain from sharing work experiences, developing a common technical language, and increasing collegial interactions. Assuming responsibility for evaluating and improving practice is fundamental to professionalism and a key to the collegial support group model of professional development. Successful support groups require time,

When skill acquisition and changed behavior are desired outcomes, complex training designs are required.

active participant involvement, administrative support, and a trained facilitator who can assist the group in developing and achieving its goals. Collegial support groups and quality circles are designs well-matched to the development of group skills, listening skills, and problem solving.

Some support groups are informal, but the most promising models seem to combine structure with flexibility. Facilitator and participant training is an important component. Adults learn how to lead and participate in groups, identify and solve problems, listen and give feedback, analyze information, and make presentations. These skills are generally applicable in relationships among adults as well as between adults and students (Hawley, 1985; La Plant, 1986; Roper & Hoffman, 1986).

Cooperative Learning

Just as cooperative learning promotes more positive attitudes toward learning and higher achievement for students (Johnson & Johnson, 1980; 1986), cooperation is an effective staff development technique for adults (Glatthorn, 1987; Pacquette, 1987). Collegial support teams, for instance, are effective in helping adults work cooperatively for mutual growth. In these groups, three to five teachers or administrators set goals of improving each others' professional competence.

Cooperative learning can also be accomplished in teams, professional dialogue, peer supervision, peer coaching, and action research. In contrast to individualistic or competitive relationships, adult cooperative learning promotes achievement, positive working relationships, motivation, participants' feelings of personal effectiveness, and a sense of shared purpose (Johnson & Johnson, 1980, 1986). Like the immediate and long-term effects of support groups, cooperative learning experiences have the potential to foster and sustain a climate of collegiality, experimentation, and interdependence.

Clinical Supervision

Unlike other supervisory relationships that emphasize performance evaluation, clinical supervision allows teachers and administrators to be learning partners. It encourages educators to determine their own focus so that they can receive support in developing and strengthening instructional skills.

The clinical supervision model follows five steps: a pre-observation conference, observation, analysis of data, post-observation conference, and evaluation of the clinical supervision process (Goldhammer, 1980). Although the supervisor is typically someone in authority, variations of the model have included peer supervision among teachers (Cogan, 1973) as well as among administrators (Peer-Assisted Leadership, 1986).

Collegial support groups help reduce isolation and improve communication, team building, collegiality, instruction, and personal and professional esteem.

Coaching

Drawing on the work of Joyce and Showers, coaching has been adapted as a staff development design. Here administrator or teacher experts demonstrate a skill that is repeated and practiced. Sometimes the practice is demonstrated in a workshop or supervisory setting; other times it is shown during an actual class. In some cases, teacher and coach work side by side and then analyze and critique the skill development together.

The concept of coaching acknowledges the complexity of transferring learning to practice. To offset that complexity, the theory and knowledge base of new techniques are explored, techniques are demonstrated and practiced, and participants receive ongoing feedback. Unlike most other professional development activities, the essence of coaching is *watching* and *practicing*, rather than *talking* (Joyce & Showers, 1982, 1983). Coaching is particularly well-suited to acquiring skills and changing behavior.

Just as peer supervision is a variation on clinical supervision, *peer coaching* is a modified form of coaching. A peer coaching design might allow two teachers or administrators learning a new skill or practice to observe each other and provide feedback, first under simulated conditions and then in the classroom. Over time and with continuing feedback, new practices become routine.

Both coaching, as a supervisory strategy, and peer coaching, as a collegial design, have the potential to build collegiality and help educators think more intently about their work. Extended coaching can enhance individual self-esteem, build self-confidence, deepen professional relationships, broaden the educator's repertoire of teaching strategies, and expand the range of learning opportunities for students.

Mentoring

Mentoring is a variation of coaching. The term was originally applied to a naturally occurring relationship between a young adult and an adult at midlife. The mentor concept has been adapted by schools and businesses to pair experienced and inexperienced adults.

A number of school systems have formal mentor programs. (Bird, 1985; Bird et al., 1985; Shulman & Hanson, 1985; Thies-Sprinthall, 1986). Mentoring involves careful screening of mentors, mentor trainers, and both new and experienced teachers. Over time, mentors observe and analyze the teaching of beginners, and both reap staff development benefits. New teachers learn to understand and analyze practice in ways that are not taught at colleges and universities. Mentors develop supervisory skills and enhance their own teaching through the teaching and learning process (Thies-Sprinthall, 1986, 1987).

Advising Teachers

The advising-teacher approach broadens the focus of collegial support to veteran as well as novice educators. Advising teachers can be lead teachers, staff developers, or specialists who work with teachers on a continuing basis. The focus of the helping relationship is

The concept of coaching acknowledges the complexity of transferring learning to practice.

determined by the teacher being helped and can range from refinement of instructional skills to developing curricula, to applying new research in the classroom.

Trainer of Trainers

Trainer-of-trainers designs have emerged out of advising teacher relationships, mentor programs, and other staff development strategies that require expertise in transferring skills and information among professionals. Once a group of teachers or administrators has become skilled in a staff development practice, participants can promote and expand the practice by training others. Not only does the training-of-trainers design require trainers to possess a complete understanding of the method to be taught, but it necessitates increasingly complex skills needed to instruct others.

A trainer-of-trainers design is a means of staff renewal as well as staff training. As they are trained and train others, participants refine old skills and learn new ones. In the process, they report a sense of energy and rekindled enthusiasm.

A trainer-of-trainers design can be a cost-effective way to expand expertise within a school or district. Having on-site trainers can also ensure the kind of close and continuing follow-up that experts from outside the school or system cannot provide. Local trainers are familiar with the setting and can adapt a practice to the specific school or district. Local participants who receive training can also increase their understanding of and commitment to the practice. Choosing skilled trainers and identifying necessary training skills are essential to the success of this approach.

Institutes

Institutes, or extended and intensive periods of staff development, are becoming increasingly popular as designs for teacher and administrator learning. The institute offers a context for in-depth learning, establishes a culture for professional renewal, and provides a setting for networking. Though school-based staff development is important, a promising feature of the institute design is its location *away from* the school. In a new setting and with new colleagues, educators have opportunities to try out ideas and behaviors. Often they find these intense learning and socializing experiences personally and professionally transforming.

Supporting the costs of institutes as well as finding convenient times when teachers and administrators can be away are important considerations. Asking participants to prepare a report or in some way share the results of the institute can help participants synthesize their learning and provide potentially relevant information to schools and districts.

Teachers' Centers, Principals' Centers, and Staff Development Centers

Teachers' centers first surfaced in the 1970s. Centers generally operate within a school or district or between collaborating organizations, such as universities or businesses. Their

---

Mentors observe and analyze the teaching of beginners, and both reap staff development benefits.

---

purpose is to respond to teacher-defined issues and concerns.

In some respects, the widespread development of principals' centers in the 1980s parallels the intentions of teachers' centers. Once the central role of the principal in school reform was reaffirmed, centers designed to bring principals together began springing up all over the country. By 1988, there were more than 120 centers in the United States and Canada (The Principals' Center, 1987).

The Wisconsin Regional Staff Development Center was started in 1978 to bring school districts and colleges together. Its programs train university faculty members, teachers, administrators, board members, and union officials from all educational levels. The Center uses a variety of collaborative staff development designs, including support groups, group discussions, and presentations. The Center has also created or used other staff development designs, such as alliances, networks, study committees, and specialized roles.

Center *alliances* are groups of school and university or college faculty members who meet regularly to share knowledge and experiences in common subject areas. Informal groups of educators who come together around mutual interests or shared problems create *networks*.

Study committees are groups of educators who analyze a professional situation and then take action. At the Wisconsin Center, for example, a committee of teachers, school board members, and administrators worked on an induction plan for new teachers. From this "Beginning Teacher Study Committee" emerged plans for a pilot induction program, a series of support seminars on issues relevant to beginning teachers, and a set of orientation guidelines for administrators. Opportunities for Wisconsin educators to take on and learn from specific Center responsibilities are termed *specialized roles*. In such roles, teachers and other educators learn to serve as mentors or develop skills such as group facilitation or grant writing (Gould & Letven, 1987).

Just as teachers' centers of the 1980s are broadening their scope, viability, and effectiveness by connecting with other school personnel, staff development centers are distinguished by their inclusiveness. Organizations that bring professionals from similar positions together and associations that connect members of the broader educational community are noteworthy staff development designs.

Networking

Networks are loosely configured groups of professionals who share a common experience, concern, or interest. They can be held together by committed and energetic individuals or, more likely, by organizations with the resources to maintain communication and provide periodic meeting places.

Networking is frequently a result of other staff development strategies. Its importance in reducing isolation and increasing professionalism suggests that more intentional linking efforts should be built into staff development designs.

As they are trained and train others, participants refine old skills and learn new ones. In the process, they report a sense of energy and rekindled enthusiasm.

Individual Study and Individually Tailored Learning

Allowing adults to determine their own learning needs and outcomes, and structuring time for their pursuit, are strategies well-matched to the increasing independence of the adult learner (see Chapter 3). Individuals can work alone on projects of their own design and be supported by others: staff developers, university faculty, advisors, learning partners, and mentors. Learners can also be supported by specific structures: learning contracts, sabbaticals, and graduate study.

Individually tailored learning can be a regular and informal method of staff development. Educators can set their own outcomes or determine them collaboratively. For example, an 11th grade English teacher became interested in mythology. The school's principal supported the teacher's new interest by helping her design a staff development agenda that included a one-week "minisabbatical" for individual study and curriculum planning and attendance at workshops throughout the year. In this case, the minisabbatical program was an ongoing professional development incentive of the district. Creating new curricula was a schoolwide objective that was supported by a series of workshops. Because the workshops were held on three mornings, the principal arranged for substitute teachers.

Professional learning does not have to be formal. Nor does it have to involve groups. The staff developer's role is to recognize individual needs and aspirations, relate them to school and district goals, and provide ongoing direction, resources, and support.

Teacher as Researcher

The teacher-as-researcher design builds on and expands the independent learning model.

Teachers can develop and respond to their own research questions in the classroom. Vivian Paley is a teacher known for her use of tape recordings, careful observation, close analysis, and lucid writing about life among children in kindergarten (Paley, 1981). Teachers can also collaborate with professional researchers to learn through active and systematic inquiry. Chapter 9 develops a cogent argument for the use of research processes and findings as goals for informed decision making.

Writing

Writing is a powerful design for staff development. Teachers and administrators can write spontaneously to unearth their thoughts and feelings on an issue. They can write from another person's perspective to gain insight into a problem or generate alternative solutions. Writing as a tool in coaching or clinical supervision can expand communication and make it more precise.

There are numerous ways to build writing into staff development. A writing group can provide teachers and administrators with a context for using writing as a way to reflect on practice. Coordination and direction from an educator trained in writing instruction and group facilitation are essential to the effectiveness of this design. During a workshop, participants can take several minutes to reflect about the topic of focus. At an institute, sustained journal writing can capture the flow of events, thoughts, and feelings.

Writing offers practitioners the time and means to reflect; it initiates and sustains professional dialogue; it fosters a sense of personal investment. The conditions that underlie effective writing and successful staff development are similar and support adult learning and growth (Levine & Jacobs, 1986).

Self-reflection and self-monitoring are parallel goals of successful staff development.

Conclusion

No one principle of adult learning will necessarily make a difference. Neither varied presentation styles nor positive external conditions for learning assure participant involvement. Successful designs for learning build upon a combination of factors to maximize involvement and participation.

Among the many conditions that support professional growth and learning, there are some essential ingredients. First, designs for learning must be predicated on research and proven practice in adult development and adult learning. All other conditions that support professional development derive from this knowledge base.

Second, effective staff development designs foster confidence in one's ability to do the job. Learning and growth start from within; adult learning is increasingly self-directed. Adults who feel in charge of and responsible for their own development will make significant gains despite seemingly insurmountable obstacles.

Third, successful professional development increases independence; it also expands the potential for collaboration. Joint effort lies at the heart of coaching, quality circles, collegial support groups, and mentor programs. Self-reflection and self-monitoring are parallel goals of successful staff development. A combination of independence and interdependence is a powerful formula for ongoing professional development and continuous school improvement.

Fourth, identifying staff development outcomes at the outset is imperative. Different outcomes require different designs. Increased effectiveness and continued personal and professional growth are overriding staff development objectives. Training designs can affect awareness, motivation, skills, knowledge, attitudes, and working climate. Staff developers must assess the outcomes of each professional development activity and use designs most likely to provide support and produce success.

Finally, successful designs for learning require time, resources, and supporting structures. Studies of change in schools and other organizations demonstrate that it can take years to institutionalize new programs and practices (Loucks-Horsley et al., 1987). Improvements are not sustained without specific systemwide commitments, support structures, and consistent monitoring.

Professional development and continuous school improvement are complex and idiosyncratic processes. Although expected patterns can be described and promising conditions can be fostered, each learning design must be tailored to individuals, schools, and districts. The design must be allowed and expected to evolve over time. Providing thoughtfully constructed staff development experiences for teachers and administrators will improve performance and professionalism for adults and expand learning opportunities for students.

Figure 5.1
Assessing Your Program

1. Which designs do we currently use and which might we add?
2. Are programs firmly grounded in adult development and adult learning theories?
3. Is there a commitment to establishing a context for growth through comfortable environments and opportunities for participation?
4. Is there recognition that lasting change takes time?
5. Is there access either to the resources and structures necessary for ongoing professional development or to support from those who have these resources?
6. Do learning designs match staff development objectives?
7. Do those responsible for staff development serve as models for continuous learning?

Figure 5.2
Competencies

Skills

1. Communication: active listening, ability to give and receive constructive feedback, questioning, writing
2. Interpersonal: group facilitation
3. Observation
4. Ability to work collaboratively
5. Modeling
6. Creativity
7. Flexibility
8. Problem solving
9. Ability to reflect on practice
10. Goal setting
11. Long-range planning
12. Techniques related to particular practices (i.e., mentoring, coaching)

Knowledge

1. Adult learning theory
2. Adult development theory
3. Staff development theory and successful practices
4. Knowledge base of teaching
5. Knowledge base of supervision

Beliefs/Attitudes

1. Adults can continue to learn and grow through their life cycles.
2. Schools must be positive learning and growing environments for children and adults.
3. Adults are most excited about their work with children when they feel positive and productive themselves.
4. Making explicit the assumptions that shape and guide our thinking and actions is an essential part of understanding ourselves and others.
5. Individuals will choose to learn and grow when the conditions for their growth and learning are appropriate.
6. Open and honest communication is one condition of a positive learning environment.
7. Successful staff development incorporates the principles of adult learning and adult growth.
8. Successful staff development fosters increased independence and interdependence.
9. Successful staff development focuses on the school as the arena for educational improvements.
10. Successful staff development requires a substantial amount of ownership, participation, and time.
11. Professional development for adults must include opportunities for a broad range of options and designs carefully matched to training objectives.

12. Adults have different learning and growing needs and styles.
13. Small, informal groups focused on shared practice can be effective vehicles for staff development.
14. Seasoned practitioners need specialized training and abilities to teach the skills of their practice.
15. Effective staff development designs foster feelings of self-efficacy, self-confidence, and self-worth.
16. Successful designs for learning require time, resources, and supporting structures.
17. Successful designs for learning build on a combination of factors to maximize involvement, ownership, and participation. No single condition of adult growth and learning necessarily makes a difference.
18. Professional development and continuous school improvement are complex and idiosyncratic processes.

References

Bird, T. (1985). *The mentor's dilemma: Prospects and demands of the California Mentor Teacher Program.* San Francisco: Far West Laboratory for Educational Research and Development.

Bird, T., Shulman, J., & Hanson, S. (1985). *Ten school districts implementing the California Mentor Teacher Program in 1984-1985.* San Francisco: Far West Laboratory for Educational Research and Development.

Cogan, M.L. (1973). *Clinical Supervision.* Boston: Houghton-Mifflin Company.

Glatthorn, A.A. (1987, Nov.). Cooperative professional development: Peer-centered options for teacher growth. *Educational Leadership, 45,* 31-35.

Goldhammer, R., Anderson, R.H., & Krajewski, R.J. (1980). *Clinical supervision: Special methods for the supervision of teachers.* (2nd Ed.) New York: Holt, Rinehart and Winston.

Gould, S., & Letven, E. (1987, Nov.). A center for interactive professional development. *Educational Leadership, 45,* 49-52.

Hawley, D. (1985). The quality circle concept. *Principal, 65*(2), 41-43.

Johnson, D.W., & Johnson, R.T. (1980, June). The key to effective inservice: Building teacher-teacher collaboration. *The Developer.*

Johnson, D.W., & Johnson, R.T. (1986). Cooperation among teachers. In David W. Johnson, Roger T. Johnson and Edythe Holubec, *Circles of learning: Cooperation in the classroom.* Englewood Cliffs, NJ: Prentice-Hall, Inc.

Joyce, B., & Showers, B. (1982, Oct.). The coaching of teaching. *Educational Leadership, 40,* 4-10.

Joyce, B., & Showers, B. (1983). *Power in staff development through research on training.* Reston, VA: Association for Supervision and Curriculum Development.

LaPlant, J. C. (1986). Collegial support for professional development and school improvement. *Theory into Practice, 25*(3), 185-190.

Levine, S., & Jacobs, V. (1986). Writing as a tool for staff development. *Journal of Staff Development, 7*(1), 44-51.

Loucks-Horsley, S., Harding, C.K., Arbuckle, M.A., Murray, L.B., Dubea, C., & Williams, M.R. (1987). *Continuing to learn: A guidebook for teacher development.* Andover, MA: The Regional Laboratory for Educational Improvement of the Northeast and Islands.

Pacquette, M. (1987, Nov.). Voluntary collegial support groups for teachers. *Educational Leadership, 45,* 36-39.

Paley, V. (1981). *Wally's stories.* Cambridge, MA: Harvard University Press.

Peer-assisted leadership: A professional development program for principals. (1986). San Francisco, CA: Far West Laboratory for Educational Research and Development.

The Principals' Center. (1987). *National directory of principals' centers.* Cambridge, MA: Harvard University, Graduate School of Education.

Roper, S.S., & Hoffman, D.E. (1986). *Collegial support for professional improvement: The Stanford collegial evaluation program.* Eugene, Oregon: School Study Council.

Shulman, J., & Hanson, S. (1985). *California mentor teacher program case study: Implementation in the Waverly Unified School District, 1984-85.* San Francisco, CA: Far West Laboratory for Educational Research and Development.

Thies-Sprinthall, L. (1986, Nov.-Dec.). A collaborative approach for mentor training: A workshop model. *Journal of Teacher Education, 37*(6), 13-20.

Thies-Sprinthall, L. (1987). *Aging teachers: Agents for revitalization and renewal as mentors and teacher educators.* Paper presented at the annual meeting of the American Education Research Association, Washington, DC.

In contrast to individualistic or competitive relationships, adult cooperative learning promotes achievement, positive working relationships, motivation, participants' feelings of personal effectiveness, and a sense of shared purpose.

Chapter 6

Continuous Improvement: Context and Support

Good workshops and release time for teachers do not necessarily ensure changes in practice for more than a few people . . . Continuous learning does not happen by chance.

Karen Kent
Jan Austin
and
Barry Kaufman

"When I decided to be a school site administrator, I had the notion that I wanted to support the learning of the teachers I worked with using all my skill, knowledge, and chutzpah. I asked myself: "How can a school be organized to focus teachers on long-term, continuous learning: refining skills, inquiring into practice, increasing autonomy, and constructing craft knowledge? . . . Workshops and seminars offered nearby provide formal opportunities for the members of my faculty. How can I take it from there?" (Austin, 1986)

Staff developers, site administrators, and district officials have come to recognize that good workshops and release time for teachers do not necessarily ensure changes in practice for more than a few people. Motivation of participants does not seem to be the primary problem, especially where voluntary participation in professional development is the norm. Internalization and transfer of learning from workshop to work place is the desired situation, but continuous learning does not just happen by chance. This chapter considers the context and practices that promote continuous learning through staff development.

Context

Context helps determine the strategies and support needed to ensure follow-up to staff development activities. The three contexts for continuous development and improvement of educators relate to students, colleagues, and the profession. To achieve continuous improvement and provide a stimulating work environment for adults, all three contexts should be supported simultaneously in staff development programs.

Students as Context

The teacher-student relationship is the core of teacher development. Teaching, a clinical profession, is organized to improve student learning and enhance human development and competence. The focus and motivation for teacher learning is on acquiring clinical skills such as classroom management, curriculum mastery, and instructional skills, as well as knowledge of content areas. When teachers continually refine skills, and update knowledge, students' school experiences are improved.

Colleagues as Context

Research suggests that a cultural norm supporting colleague interaction contributes to more effective school practice (Little, 1984; Rosenholtz, 1987). However, educators are often isolated from one another with minimal time and money available to exchange, discuss, coach, think out loud, and test ideas.

The primary task in the colleague-centered context is to translate what is learned in workshops to what happens in the school and the classroom. A school that supports inquiry into practice allows for exploring and disseminating ideas. Whether studying or reporting on curriculum reforms, evaluating teaching practices, talking about teacher leadership roles, participating in school decisions, or working with new or prospective teachers, educators can expand and clarify their own knowledge and practice while contributing to collective professional knowledge.

Profession as Context

Involvement in issues advancing the profession is an often-overlooked context for the professional development of teachers and administrators. The norm in medicine, law, and mental health allows for allocation of resources for case conferences. These conferences include exchanging and analyzing clinical material, case literature, and case studies as well as generating hypotheses. In this respect, teachers and site administrators are presently an underused resource for the advancement of practical knowledge about teaching and learning.

Practices to Stimulate and Promote
Continuous Improvement

Teachers should be learners. They should be continuously refining their skills. They should become more and more autonomous. They should take leadership in school issues regarding teaching and learning. They should collaborate with each other and the principal to manage dilemmas and solve problems. They should teach and coach each other and the principal. They should expect all of the above from the principal. (Austin, 1986)

Three conditions are necessary to bring about continuous improvement of schooling.

1. School districts must value and aspire to reach optimal conditions for teachers and administrators to develop their professional competence. Evidence of optimal conditions would be found in such actions as keeping districtwide declarations to a minimum, involving teachers in developing district curriculum, decentralizing budgets (except for personnel and maintenance), encouraging site administrators to involve teachers in the site-budgeting process, providing professional development and curriculum staff members or providing access to people who can be used as resources at the school sites on a regular basis, and providing a professional library and encouraging its regular use.

2. Schools must be organized to be places for ongoing growth and development of students, teachers, and administrators. The site-budgeting process should allocate funds to provide time for teachers and administrators for observing and coaching; for participating in workshops, training programs, and professional conferences; and for working with other professionals or resource people. Faculty meetings should include time for thoughtful discussion of important professional issues as well as for problem solving or decision making. Faculty representatives should actively participate in decisions involving school budget, suspending students, and staff development, to mention only a few.

3. Professionals should expect to work together to:

* Refine practice.
* Adopt state-of-the-art practices for teaching specific subjects.
* Develop and share knowledge and information about the crafts of teaching and administration.
* Increase their knowledge of student growth and development.
* Adjust their expectations according to student needs.
* Provide challenging learning environments.

The public may assume that these conditions already are in place. but typically, they are not. Occasionally barriers arise from tacit agreements among teachers inhibit them from exploring their own growth. (Principals often hold similar assumptions.)

* Teachers work privately behind their classroom doors. When students are present, colleagues do not enter the classroom except under urgent circumstances.
* Teachers believe they must be practical by making sure the "basics" are covered. A touch of enrichment is more than one person can accomplish in 180 days of instruction. This notion is tied to the generally held assumption that the textbooks must be completed and that a teacher's job is teaching students. Everything else is an add-on that can be done if there is time and energy before or after the regular school day.

* Accountability is the principal's job.
* The only way teachers can learn is by trial and error.
* Research is for college professors. It is not for practitioners because it really does not make much sense.

Role Groups: Actors and Supporters

If staff developers are to be the change agents for schools and districts, they need knowledge that will help create conditions for continuous improvement of teaching. This process involves various players who, in this discussion, are called role groups. According to their functions, these role groups can be categorized as actors or supporters:

* Actors include those who are expected to be at the hub of the action. This group consists of teachers, site administrators, and school staff members. These are the people who are in daily contact with students and communicate directly with the parents of those students.
* There are two groups of supporters. Institutional, or organizational, supporters set the direction and priorities and provide financial and policy support for schools. This group is composed of district administrators, school board members, parents, community leaders, and professional organization leaders.

Technical supporters provide specialized knowledge and skill-training and offer planning assistance. This group includes staff developers, teacher educators from institutions of higher education, and curriculum and instruction leaders.

The primary task in the colleague-centered context is to translate what is learned in workshops to what happens in the school and the classroom.

Functions of Actors and Supporters

"Actors": The Teachers. In schools that are developing conditions for continuous improvement, faculties are composed of teachers who collaborate with principals or superintendents. Their functions include:

* Taking collegial work from conception to action.
* Promoting collaborative projects, which could include exploring the variety of ways to use manipulatives in a math program or examining practices that challenge students' higher-order thinking skills.
* Contacting resource people for assistance in planning and executing projects.
* Planning the use of new curriculum materials, revisions of student assessment, and use of technology in the curriculum.
* Leading discussions on problems and needs.
* Questioning present practices, rationales and directions.
* Collecting and scrutinizing student and school data.
* Enlisting other resource people to explore new approaches in curriculum, teaching methods, and subject matter.

* Becoming knowledgeable about research based on teaching practice.
* Sharing findings and experiences with colleagues through workshops, seminars, or collaborative work.
* Being open to evaluating and trying out new ideas, (i.e., the use of recommended computer software to support instruction in a content area).
* Helping to create systems for working together, trying them out in classrooms, evaluating progress, and reporting results.
* Working with site and district administrators to provide time for refining and improving teaching practice during teacher workdays and to arrange pay for teachers' time outside of the normal workday as needed.

"Actors": The Principals. Tasks and functions of site administrators would include:
* Providing the leadership for teachers to participate in these activities.
* Appearing regularly in classrooms to observe students and teaching (thanking the teacher for the opportunity; discussing observations with the teacher).
* Making positive comments to teachers about their classroom skills.
* Posing questions for teachers to reflect upon and discuss (i.e., "What teacher behaviors calm a child who brings the emotions of a chaotic home to school?" "What teacher behaviors inspire and motivate students to initiate their own learning?" "What is different about this year's class? Why aren't they responding to the Moon Watching Unit like last year's class?"). The basic question underlying these inquiries is, "How can we get better at what we do?"
* Supplying leadership for collaborative decision making by the faculty (i.e., about curriculum and instruction).
* Mediating discussions among staff members.
* Participating with teachers in selected professional-development activities.
* Working with staff developers to develop school-based peer coaching, teacher seminars, and site workshops based on faculty initiatives.
* Monitoring and assisting the coordination of faculty work and communicating the process and results to district administrators.
* Advocating faculty and school needs to groups that provide support.

"Supporters": The School Boards and District Administrators. These groups show commitment to teacher professional work through:
* Developing and adopting policies that legitimize teacher collegial work.
* Allocating resources to provide time for teacher collaboration by extending teacher workdays or workyears, sharing contract arrangements, or allowing the more traditional arrangement of release time.
* Advocating to parents and the community the importance and benefits of teacher professional growth and development.
* Recognizing and rewarding teachers and site administrators for collaborative projects that advance the teaching profession and promote teacher growth and development.

"Supporters": The University and Other Curriculum and Staff Development Personnel. These groups offer support through:
* Working with teachers and administrators to identify needs and goals.
* Being on site.
* Leading or participating in staff planning meetings or bringing together teacher leaders with common interests to identify needs and goals.

* Building into the training design the expectation that follow-up activities will take place. Such activities might include:
  1. Monthly or bimonthly meetings or workshops to share progress and problems or to discuss adaptations of a practice.
  2. A designated number of coaching and conference sessions with a trainer.
  3. School-based workshops to teach peer coaching techniques that could be used in conjunction with the original training.
  4. Site-based seminars led by teacher-participants for other teachers in the school to increase awareness of the topic.
  5. Videotaped sample lessons to be shared by teacher-participants with others as a basis for discussing a lesson. In the beginning these sessions should be led by an experienced staff developer.
  6. Regular seminars with teachers to reflect on practice, using questions from workshops or training sessions, from the staff developer, or from their own group.
  7. Providing participants with a structure for regular journal-keeping to be used as a basis for follow-up workshops, meetings, or seminars.
  8. Providing teachers with opportunities to visit others who share professional interests or values but who teach in different schools, grade levels, or subject areas. Opportunity should be provided for conversation between the teacher visited and the visiting teacher.

Teachers and site administrators are presently an underused resource for the advancement of practical knowledge about teaching and learning.

---

* Supplying translations of teaching-practice research into practical methods applicable by teachers and administrators. Incorporate research into workshops, seminars, news-letters, and informal professional exchanges. Circulate copies of articles or papers to people who have expressed an interest.
* Aiding teacher collaboration by structuring time and providing needed materials or information.
* Providing starting points for teachers, collectively or individually, to inquire into the purpose and effects of their own practice.
* Introducing and modeling cooperative learning structures for students and teachers.
* Teaching administrators and teachers up-to-date content knowledge and state-of-the-art pedagogical knowledge.
* Providing information on and training to use materials and technology that enhance instruction and student learning.
* Aiding teachers and administrators in developing coaching and other collegial systems. Many peer coaching models have been developed that can be used until a beginner becomes more competent and can refine the process to make it work better. (Excellent

reviews of this type of work appear in the spring 1987 issue of *The Journal of Staff Development*.)

* Contributing feedback, if requested, to school faculties.

Relations between Actors and Supporters

The functions and responsibilities of these groups, although distinct, overlap in numerous areas. Through cooperation and collaboration, they can strengthen their assigned roles. This requires meeting and discussing issues as well as sharing ideas and knowledge. Moreover, all groups need to allow the lines that traditionally separate them to blur occasionally. At times, new lines of decision making may need to be drawn.

Implied, although not mentioned above, is the impact of actors and supporters on students. Students are the subjects through whom current methods are refined and new ones are tested. Ultimately, effects on students are the key to measuring the quality of an educational endeavor. Teachers and parents sometimes wonder if students know that schools are supposed to be places for learning. A powerful way to communicate this message is for teachers and administrators to be models of learning as well as teaching. So the school becomes a place of learning for all.

Figure 6.1
Assessing Your Program: Do You Provide for
Continuous Learning?

1. How is ongoing professional learning integrated into the yearly goal statements and ongoing supervision practices at the school site and in the district?
2. What has been done to create time for collegial exchange and reflection?
3. How much time is allocated in grade level and faculty meetings to discuss school concerns or issues, progress of activities, and to solve problems that affect the whole faculty?
4. Has a districtwide calendar of professional development activities been developed and distributed?
5. Is there regular communication to parents about the professional development activities of the faculty? Has a clear rationale been given for the use of substitutes to create released time?
6. What is the budget at the school level to support participation in professional development activities by the principal and faculty? Have they had a hand in planning the activities?

Conclusion

There has been a consistent concern that schools and classrooms are not places where students are motivated, able learners. Nor are schools viewed as stimulating, interesting environments for adults. Moreover, in this period of technological and informational revolution, many feel that the school is becoming less relevant.

As one principal noted:

> *The teachers in my school attend many workshops, more than teachers from any other school in the district. I make sure they are informed of the workshops offered by a staff development consortium that the district joins each year, by two science museums, by the state department, colleges and universities and other professional workshops put on by consultants. Most of these learning opportunities occur during the school day and require release time. Teachers experience that going to a workshop is not an "add on" to their professional work. They had to declare that their learning was important enough for them to be away from their students. As teachers assume responsibility of learning as part of their professional work, they realize that some of their classroom work could be done effectively by someone else. They plan the days they're away so that it isn't just a "day on hold" for the students. Now substitutes want to come to our school, because they often have leeway to extend an ongoing classroom activity that they might be able to see the next time. We're creating a school environment that promotes learning opportunities for all, including substitutes.*
>
> *I deal incisively with parents' attitudes about teachers being away at workshops during the school day. I have an explicit goal educating parents to expect our school to provide continuous learning opportunities for all teachers. I assert that modeling is the most powerful instructional tool: it is imperative that every adult in the school is a learner. (Austin, 1986)*

The school can provide the context for growth as a process — not an event. All groups must be committed to study, support, and implement both present and future developments in professional teaching practices. Continuous refinement and improvement of practice should be the norm. Students should be provided with models for learning and functioning that enable the world of the future.

I assert that modeling is the most powerful instructional tool; it is imperative that every adult in the school is a learner.

References

Austin, J. (1984-86). *Journals of a Principal*. Unpublished document.

Little, J.W. (1982). Norms of collegiality and experimentation: Workplace conditions of school success. *American Educational Research Journal, 19*, 325-340.

Rosenholtz, S. (1987, April). *Organizational conditions of teaching*. Paper presented at the Annual Meeting of the American Educational Research Association, Washington DC.

Chapter 7

Assessing Program Effects

A good evaluation documents the value of staff development as measured by its impoact on both staff members and the students they serve.

Jon C. Marshall

Patton (1982) and Little (1982) both point out the essential criterion for good staff development evaluation: It should be useful. The evaluation should provide information that helps collegial planning and delivery of staff development. Moreover, it should doucment the value of staff development as measured by its impact on staff members and the students they serve.

What makes for a useful evaluation? Not methodolgical excellence, timeliness, findings, or level of outcomes. The two factors that actually determine whether an evaluation is used are political considerations, such as those related to continued funding, and whether the evaluation was planned from the beginning of the program with the intention of being used (Patton, 1982). If neither factor is present, the quality of the evaluation is moot. If these factors are present, however, the evaluation is likely to be used regardless of its quality.

More than 100 evaluation approaches have been proposed in the literature. These can be grouped into about eight models, four of which are useful for staff developers: case study model, systems model, goal-based model, and quasi-legal model.

The choice of an evaluation model depends on the audience, what prompts the evaluation, how data is collected, and how results are used. For staff development evaluations, the model should match the audience. Typically, for a program staff, the case study model is used; for program coordinators or funding agencies, systems or goal-based models are used. The quasi-legal model is used for school boards of education or professional panels.

Evaluation Components

An evaluation of a staff development program involves three types of activites: specifying what is to be evaluated, assuring that the program is working as intended, and choosing a method for determining the results of the program. The latter activity can have four components: the specific results expected from the program, standards for judging the results, instrumentation for collecting data, and procedures for analyzing the data.

Formative evaluation focuses only on the first two types of evaluation, with primary concern for clarifying what is to be evaluated. The focus is on the process of program implementation. The case study provides formative information.

Summative evaluation involves adding to evaluation the third type of activity focusing on staff development program outcomes. System models, goal-based models, and quasi-legal models, usually focus on program outcomes.

Evaluation Models

For each of these four models, there are identifiable advocates and practitioners, extensive literature, and completed evaluations and an explicit, idealized rationale. The procedures used depend on the questions (Patton, 1982) and the audience served (House, 1981). Frequently, it may be appropriate to use more than one model when conducting an evaluation.

Figure 7.1 classifies the four evaluation models. House (1981) and Hales (1986) were drawn upon heavily for this taxonomy.

Case Study

Case studies show what a program looks like from the viewpoints of the staff developers and the participating educators. The idea is to describe and evaluate the staff development program by investigating the needs, values, and perceptions of its audiences (Worthen & Sanders, 1973). Target audiences for a case-study evaluation typically are those with an interest in the staff development program (Stake, 1973): the coordinator of staff development, other staff developers, building and central office administrators, and teachers.

The case study is characterized by "thick description." It involves naturalistic research strategies, including participant observation, unstructured interviews, document analysis and, perhaps, limited use of surveys (Alkins, Daillak & White, 1979). This process is

Figure 7.1
Evaluation Models

Characteristic	Model			
	Case Study	Systems	Goal-Based	Quasi-Legal
Primary Audience	Client; Program Staff	Managers; Funding Agencies	Managers; Fund- Agencies	Panel; Jury
Consensus Assured for	Negotiated Activities	Overall Goals; Hypotheses; Serialized Outcomes	Program Behavioral Objectives; Specific Outcomes	Rules; Procedures; Panel; Judge
Methodology	Ethnographic Methods; Participant Observation; Unstructured Interview; Document Analysis; Simple Survey	Hypothesis Testing; Experimental Design; Cost- Benefit Analysis; Testing; Comparative Survey	Numerative Analysis; Hypothesis Testing; Document Review; Testing; Survey	Advocacy Preparation Quasi-Legal Procedures
Outcomes	"Thick Description" Understand- ing; Clarification	Efficiency; Cost- Benefit; Effectiveness	Task-Analy- sis; Project Specific; Productivity; Accountability	Jury Decision; Resolution
Typical Questions	What does the program look like from the staff and participants' points of view?	What is the most effective program? Can the effects of the program be general- ized?	Are the program objectives being met? Is the program do- ing what it claimed it would do?	What are the arguments for the program?

democratic and involves continuous negotiation among the evaluator, audiences, and participants. The data for the evaluation usually take the form of extensive field notes and interviews. As this information is synthesized by the researcher, the results often are fed back to the participants for verification. Establishing evaluation validity and objectivity rests upon the professional skills of the evaluator, the use of participant groups to provide perceptual checks, and a clearly written report.

Good case-study evaluation is time-consuming and costly. However, when the primary interest is in understanding how the staff development program is being implemented and how participants are perceiving the program, the case study is a promising formative evaluation model.

The main weakness of case study evaluation is directly associated with its strength: The interpersonalization inherent in a good case study can endanger evaluator objectivity and evaluation validity. The evaluator can easily become too involved in the situation. Case study evaluation requires that the evaluator be trained in naturalistic research methods and basic statistics. Although evaluators can be mentors to staff development program coordinators, evaluators must remain separate from program decision making. Case study evaluation is not a one-shot, "quickie" report on a program; rather, it is a long-term documentation of a program from the participants' points of view. Quickie case-study evaluations are likely to convey misinformation that can cause irreparable damage to a staff development program.

The choice of an evaluation model depends on the audience, what prompts the evaluation, how data is collected, and how results are used.

Case Example 1. The Schenley High Teachers' Center in Pittsburgh has used extensive evaluation, including documentation, formative evaluation, and impact evaluation (Cooley & Bickel, 1986; Denton & LeMahieu, 1985; Hovey, 1986; Johnson & Brandt, 1986). The documentation and formative activities best represent case study evaluation. One study involved observing teachers before and after experience with the Teachers' Center. The data indicated that after attending the staff development program, teachers spent more time teaching, gave students more positive feedback, and spent more time on task. In contrast, teachers spent less time on behavior management and transitional activities.

In another study, extensive interview and survey data came from examining the roles of visiting and resident teachers. Both strengths and weaknesses of these roles were documented and acted upon in program planning.

Case Example 2. "Practical Realities for School-Based Staff Development" (Wood, Caldwell, & Thompson, 1986), illustrates case study methodology. In discussing program audits, the authors state

> *Our audit team analyzed documents and conducted extensive interviews with*
> *central office administrators . . . ,principals, teachers, representatives of the*

teachers' organizations, and, of course staff developers . . . .The focus was on discovering as much as we could about current practice and the perceptions of district personnel about school-based improvement and effective staff development . . .

The audits provided the district with answers to several important questions:
* What organizational context is required for school-based improvement?
* What is the role and the mission of staff development within this context?
* What staff development practices are most appropriate to support school-based improvement?
* How should staff development be organized and managed to facilitate school-based improvement goals and plans?
* What training programs will be necessary for central office personnel, principals, teachers, and staff developers as they begin school-by-school improvement? (pp. 54-55)

Note that all questions addressed by the audit team were focused on clarification at the formative evaluation level, the level most appropriate to the case study.

The case study is characterized by "thick description" including participant observation, unstructured interviews, document analysis and, perhaps, limited use of surveys.

Systems Evaluation

Systems evaluation is used to learn whether staff development programs have the best possible structure, distribute their resources and functions optimally, and work efficiently (Doctors & Wokutch, 1980). This evaluation emphasizes outcomes. It applies an industrial economic) production model to staff development, with efficiency of program delivery as a primary goal (Apple, 1974). One emphasis of a systems evaluation is the cost-benefit. It is assumed that increased monetary returns are beneficial, and that market prices are appropriate value measures (Doctors & Wokutch, 1980). The purpose, then, for doing a systems evaluation is to assure some maximum results from a staff development program (McLaughlin, 1975). The idea is to maximize the good arising from staff development through one overall index of program effectiveness (Hales, 1986).

This approach to evaluation was developed in the Department of Defense under Secretary Robert McNamara using microeconomic theory. During the mid-1960s it was embraced by the Department of Health, Education, and Welfare (HEW) and became the primary mode for evaluating programs funded through Titles I and IV of the Elementry and Secondary Education Act (ESEA). RMC Research Corporation shepherded the systems evaluation movement for the Title I programs by developing methods for aggregating evaluation data across districts. Title III and, subsequently, Title IV programs depended on states implementing this federal movement. To accomplish this, an elaborate scheme was devised, consisting of third-party evaluators, evaluation audits, state validation, and federal validation through the Joint Dissemination Review Panel (JDRP). The target audiences for such systems evaluations are the funding agency and other appropriate administrators (Rossi, Freeman, & Write, 1979).

The primary method for systems evaluation is experimental or quasi-experimental design. Planned variations in program design are preferred to naturally occurring variations (Cooley & Lohnes, 1976). Data are collected using surveys, tests, and structured interviews keyed to specific research hypotheses. When using this model, it is generally assumed that there is a small set of questions that every evaluator should ask when evaluating a program.

For example, to evaluate a staff development program focusing on strategies for teaching writing, the evaluator should determine whether the program led to improved writing among students of the trained teachers. A systems evaluation would consist of pretesting and posttesting student writing achievement for the trained teachers and a matched group of untrained teachers. Ideally, the evaluator would first randomly place teachers into the staff development program; second, test student writing achievement immediately after teacher training and again several months later; and, third, evaluate the achievement test results,

The ultimate goal in systems evaluation is to establish a cause-and-effect relation and thus be able to generalize the evaluation findings.

looking for a significant pretest- posttest difference by trained vs. untrained group interaction in a repeated measure factorial analysis.

The ultimate goal in this type of evaluation is to establish a cause-and-effect relation and thus be able to generalize the evaluation findings. This goal spurred the Department of Education's efforts to establish demonstration programs that have passed rigorous systems review.

The weakness of the systems evaluation model rests on the assumption that staff developers and others can agree on the goals of staff development. Can a single, ideal set of results be defined? Or is staff development a pluralistic concept? The problem of identifying a unified definition can be seen in two ongoing debates. Is staff development designed to maintain ''good educators'' or to upgrade ''poor educators.'' Should it be held responsible for changes in educators or for changes in students?

Another concern is that systems evaluations can provide accountability information for funding agencies yet have little impact on local programs except for their continued funding.

Case Example 1. Judith Little (1982) describes using a systems evaluation to assess staff development programs.

> *This (staff development) program was intended to constitute the strongest possible test of a set of ideas based on recent research on effective instruction.*

To test their ideas, program designers asked teachers to learn and apply a set of ideas and practices in their classrooms. Volunteers were randomly assigned to experimental and control groups and students were assigned to heterogeneous classes. Program planners then designed a set of . . . measures and methods that offered several sources and types of data on classroom implementation and student impact. These included periodic classroom observations in experimental and control classes to determine differences in instructional approach over the project period. They also included pre- and post-test measures of student performance, peer relations, behavior and attachment to school. (p. 39)

Little described the following possible results of staff development evaluation:
* gain in participants' knowledge or skills
* favorable attitudes toward specific perspectives or practices
* increase in the frequency and rigor with which recommended practices are actually used
* expanded number and range of persons, groups or buildings attempting promising practices
* strengthened commitment to testing and continuing effective practices
* improved willingness to examine, alter, or abandon old practices and to test new ones; willingness to expose knowledge, skills and experience to the scrutiny of others
* widened tolerance for the struggle required to improve practice, and expanded administrator or collegial support and assistance in doing so
* strengthened sense of confidence or efficacy with respect to specific ideas or generally with respect to the prospects for doing a good job
* broadened and strengthened belief in the ability of children to learn and the ability of teachers to teach them; a related belief that good teachers and principals are made, not born
* demonstrated ability and willingness to work collaboratively or collegially to improve classroom or school practices (p. 27)

Clearly, Little's criteria, if fully operational, would maximize the good of staff development. These results could form the basis for effective systems evaluation.

The focus of goal-based evaluation is on the targeted goals for a specific staff development program in terms of program activities and procedures.

Case Example 2. Marshall & Caldwell (1982) describe a computer-based evaluation and management process based on systems evaluation assumptions. The process began with agreement on goals at the district- and school-levels. Then, teachers needs were assessed, teacher participation in inservice programs was monitored, and teachers evaluated the degree to which inservice objectives were met. Continuing reassessment was made of inservice needs. As a result, individual and inservice program information could be examined, enabling program coordinators to determine cost benefits of staff development programs. Specific experimental methodologies for program evaluations were described. Teachers provided most of the data, although the effect on students was examined in few of the studies. This staff development evaluation model is clearly an attempt to use systems methods to maximize staff development effectiveness.

In goal-based evaluations, it is clear that all three questions should be asked about staff development objectives: Is the program objective of value? Is the objective technically sound and feasible? Has the objective actually been put into practice?

Case Example 3. Applying a cost-effective model to staff development is illustrated by Simmons (1982). She described a six-stage model for determining the relative cost effectiveness of alternative staff development activities. She claimed that use of this model would increase the quality and quantity of information available to staff development coordinators for program planning. She pointed out that:

> *Cost-effectiveness analysis methodology is based on the assumption that dollars are an adequate standardized measure of cost. However, even if the salaries of two different training leaders are the same, their effectiveness and the effectiveness of their programs may vary tremendously. In this way, dollars can be a very misleading measure of the program inputs or cost. (This underscores the point that program evaluation results are truly situation-specific and not generalizable.)*
> *A second problem involves the difficulty of accurately determining trainer and participant time inputs to a program . . . .As a related issue, the time which program participants invest in a training activity is frequently not accurately measured or even considered as a relevant item in the cost-side of the analysis. (pp. 143-144)*

Goal-Based Evaluation

A goal-based evaluation determines if the stated objectives for a staff development program have been met. The idea is similar to that advocated in the systems model of striving to maximize good through an overall index of program effectiveness. The primary difference in the goal-based model is that the focus of the evaluation is on the targeted goals for a specific staff development program rather than some general, presumed functions for all staff development programs. The goals can be stated in terms of program outcomes or in terms of program activities and procedures.

Goal-based evaluation relieves the evaluator of the problem of determining the criteria for program effectiveness. These criteria are already specified in the program objectives.

The task of the evaluator is simply to determine whether the objectives have been met.

The evaluator must be able to establish the logical links from the conceptual program model, as reflected in the program goals, through the program implementation, to the empirical data collected (Stake, 1976). Consequently, one must either link results directly to the program goals or determine whether failure to obtain results is a result of inappropriate theory or poor program implementation. This concept is illustrated by Shapiro (1985) using Stake's (1976) Model of Contingency and Congruence for a worksite program in health and science.

The target audience for goal-based evaluation often is staff development program coordinators. The purpose is to provide feedback to program personnel for improving the staff development program (Doctors & Wokutch, 1980). Through efforts of federal programs like Title IV of ESEA and Bilingual Grants, the goal-based model has become one of the major modes for reporting to federal funding agencies. Frequently it has been difficult to distinguish between systems and goal-based models for reporting. For goal-based evaluation, the specific goals (often hypotheses) are specified as part of program planning and are unique to the staff development program being evaluated.

The purpose of quasi-legal evaluation is to determine staff development program quality through adversarial hearings.

The key element in a goal-based evaluation is specifying behavioral objectives. Objectives typically are defined in one of the following ways:

* After completing the staff development program, teachers will demonstrate at least an 80% mastery of technique "X" as measured by the Technique "X" Assessment Test.
* After completing the staff development program, teachers will demonstrate at least a 10% growth in their understanding of technique "X" as measured by the Technique "X" Assessment Test administered immediately before and after the staff development program.
* After completing the staff development program, teachers will demonstrate significantly p .05 greater gains in understanding of technique "X" than an untreated control group of teachers as measured by the Technique "X" Assessment Test administered immediately before and after the staff development program.
* After completing the staff development program, at least 65% of the participating teachers will be using treatment "X" in their classroom, as verified through the Treatment "X" Observation Schedule administered 6- to 10-weeks after the completion of the program.

The primary weaknesses of the goal-based model are twofold. First, there often is no opportunity for the evaluation to address adequacy of the objectives. Second, the objectives can easily become trivialized. When the evaluation is an "add-on" requirement of an outside funding agency, it sometimes becomes a formality that is of little value to anyone.

These problems can be avoided by asking three critical questions about the value of the program objective. First, whom does it benefit? Second, are both the idea and approach for reaching the objective sound and feasible? Third, has there been real change in practice that indicates that the objective actually has been implemented (adapted from Fullan, 1982)? Figure 7.2 presents a schematic for the eight possible groups of answers when these questions are asked in a goal-based evaluation. These answers illustrate why staff development programs should be continually monitored. Type I is the result that staff development program coordinators strive for: The program objective is of value; it has technical quality in that it is sound and feasible; and the objective actually has been implemented. Type V, however, reflects a planning problem. Here a highly valued, technically feasible objective has not been implemented. Type II suggests poor conceptual development of the objective: A highly valued objective is poorly developed so that it is implemented, although technically unsound. In short, a good idea has become a bad staff development program. The Type IV outcome is one that every staff development coordinator hopes to avoid: A non-valued objective that is technically unsound is actually implemented.

Figure 7.2
Types of implementation outcomes for staff development programs.

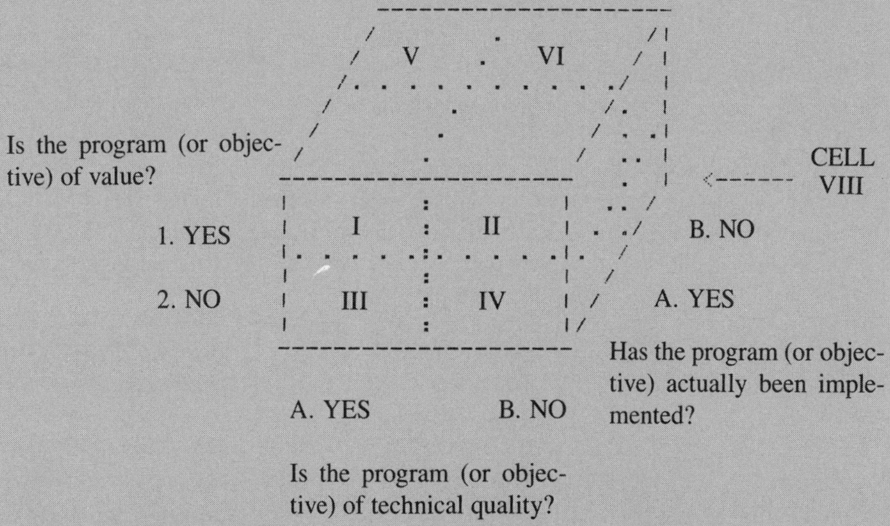

In many goal-based evaluations, only the third question — whether the objective has been implemented — is addressed. This practice has been common since the 1960s for evaluating innovative educational programs funded by federal or state governments. It is clear, though, that all three questions should be asked about staff development objectives: Is the program objective of value? Is the objective technically sound and feasible? Has the objective actually been put into practice?

Whether a case is won or lost may depend upon the skill with which the evaluator presents the evidence rather than the actual effectiveness of the staff development program.

Case Example 1. An article by Ryan and Crowell (1982) provides steps for planning a goal-based evaluation.
1. Define program goals in terms of measurable processes and results.
2. Identify indicators that goals are being met.
3. Identify tests for documenting presence and nature of indicators.
4. Identify designers for tests or of existing tests.
5. Identify collectors or monitors of the data.
6. Identify dates for making evaluative decisions.
7. Identify data analysis procedures.
8. Identify value judgements to be made and appropriate criteria for making them. (p. 167)

Some of the evaluation questions that Ryan and Crowell identified were:
* Do teachers acquire knowledge and skills to improve student learning and performance as identified through the needs assessment and program development process?
* Do teachers achieve professional and personal goals as identified through the needs assessment and program development process?
* Did the activity lead to the adoption of new or changed behaviors?
* Do the participants use the new skills, new curriculum, or new processes?
* Do participants perceive that the program has improved their performance?
* Was it informative and useful to the participants?
* Do administrators perceive that performance of participants has been improved? (p. 167)

Although these question are general, they easily could be written as behavioral objectives.

Case Example 2. The information management system (Marshall & Caldwell, 1982) cited earlier relied on both goal-based and systems methodologies. Program planning had incorporated both teacher-needs assessment and systematic program evaluation, using goal-based procedures.

Two weeks to a month prior to an inservice program, the program planners determine the objectives, topic classification, and any test items to be administered. Staff members, who indicated an interest in the topic . . . are invited to attend, ...and evaluation forms are preprinted with the program title, topics, and objectives.

At the beginning of the first session, participants are asked to complete the identification section on the evaluation form and to review information on the topic and objectives of the session . . . .

If a pretest is administered, the responses are marked on the front of the form. At the close of the program, participants rate the degree to which the objectives were met, the quality of the program and leader . . . .Any posttest responses are marked on the back of the form.

Once a month, all completed evaluation forms are scanned and entered into the computer system. At this point, any of several data reports can be computer-generated for utilization by program planners. (pp. 88-89)

A computer-based system was used to generate information specific to the goals and objectives of the staff development program. Staff development coordinators could use this information for program planning. This exemplifies the primary purpose for goal-based evaluation.

A program coordinator who also is the program evaluator has maximum control over the flow and use of information. However, it is often difficult for someone directly involved to be objective in determining informational needs or interpreting information.

Case Example 3. Marshall (1988) reported on the effects of a tiered staff development model that has been used to train elementary and secondary teachers in methods of teaching writing. The training program was implemented in several districts located in different regions of the United States. The evaluation procedure for this staff development program was a combination of systems and goal-based techniques using an approach recommended by Stake (1967). Taken into consideration in this evaluation were the pre-conditions for program implementation, program characteristics, and program impact.

The program evaluation consisted of the following steps.

Step 1: Determination of the degree to which all the pre-conditions had been met. This was done through the examination of program records and staff interviews.

Step 2: Documentation that the staff development activities had been implemented as specified. This was done through the examination of records, conducting on-site visits, and analysis of participant program evaluation forms.

Step 3: Assessment of the pre- and post-behaviors of the teachers to determine direct program outcomes. The behaviors examined were: (1) perceived levels of behavior prior to and immediately after the staff development program and (2) types of teaching procedures used in the classroom several months after completing the staff development program, as compared to control teachers.

Step 4: Documentation of outcomes of the staff development program by pre- and posttesting students on writing achievement.

Students of teachers attending the staff development program were compared to students of teachers not participating in the program. By linking differences in student achievement back to differences in teaching procedures that could be linked back to participation in the staff development program, a strong causal-comparative case was able to be made for the significance of the staff development program impact. In fact, it was able to be shown that the staff development program had effect sizes of .42 at the elementary level, .61 at the middle school level, and .28 at the high school level.

Quasi-Legal Evaluation

The purpose of this model is to determine staff development program quality through adversarial hearings. The assumption is that the best evidence will prevail if each side in the hearing strives, in partisan fashion, to present to the jury the most favorable evidence for its side (Owens, 1973).

Panels that hear the evidence derive their authority from quasi-legal procedures. Evidence is submitted. The hearings are marked by courtroom symbolism and solemnity. Even the room used to hold the hearings may take on a courtroom appearance (House, 1981). The program evaluator acts as defense attorney for the staff development program. The chair of the panel frequently acts as the prosecutor. Typically, both the prosecutor and the panel members are allowed to question the evaluator on any aspect of the evaluation. The final decision rests on a majority vote of the panel, which serves as the jury. An example of this model might be the presentation of a program evaluation to a school board.

Another form of quasi-legal evaluation uses an assigned prosecutor apart from the panel. In this case, the panel may consist of three-to-five judges who will decide the merits of the case. Actual witnesses might be called to testify. Again, the evaluator has the role of the defense attorney.

Note that in this model the focus is on presenting the best evidence in a legalistic, adversarial manner. This assumes a known structure for presenting arguments and inferences to keep the evaluation intellectually honest and fair (Wolf, 1975). The evaluator must collect and prepare evidence consistent with the set of rules established by the panel. As in legal hearing, knowing the rules of the system may be the most important skill. Data preparation most likely will emulate that of the systems or goal-based evaluation models.

The main weakness of the quasi-legal format might also be viewed as its strength. Whether a case is won or lost may depend upon the skill with which the evaluator presents the evidence rather than the actual effectiveness of the staff development program.

Case Example 1. The Joint Dissemination Review Panel JDRP within the Department of Education offers one of the best examples of the use of the quasi-legal evaluation model in education. The panel hears evidence and decides whether or not educational programs are eligible for federal monies to disseminate them to districts throughout the country.

For instance, the JDRP heard the case for a writing project based on a training-of-trainers staff development model. A goal-based evaluation model had been used with the objectives written in the form of statistical hypotheses. Data were presented on several thousand students. A consultant who had successfully defended other projects before the JDRP was hired to advise the program evaluator on presenting the evidence. A few weeks before the hearing, the program director submitted a written evaluation report to the U. S. Office of Education for review by panel members. The report followed a format specifically required for JDRP hearings.

The internal evaluator is responsible for gathering information on district, school, and staff needs as well as program participation and program effectiveness.

The actual hearing was conducted in formal legal fashion using a panel of professional staff drawn from the National Institute of Education and the U.S. Office of Education. The panel asked questions about the written evidence of the program director and evaluator, who answered only "yes" or "no", providing no voluntary explanations. Based on the evidence, the panel voted unanimously to validate the program. This writing program was again validated by the panel in 1986. The evaluation data for the program presented at the second appearance before the JDRP are in a paper by Pritchard and Marshall (1987).

The Program Evaluator

Who evaluates a program depends on the size and budget of the staff development program. In many programs, the staff development coordinator has several roles, including program evaluator. In other programs, a separate staff member can be employed to serve as an evaluator. In still other programs, an outside evaluator will be used. There are advantages and disadvantages to each arrangement.

A program coordinator who also is the program evaluator has maximum control over the flow and use of information. That person develops information collection devices, collects and analyzes the data, and uses the information as needed. Intimacy with the information allows the program coordinator to make the best possible use of it. The drawbacks of this approach stem from this intimacy. It is often difficult for someone directly involved to be objective in determining informational needs or interpreting information. In addition, coordinators must take care not to get so caught up in daily administrative tasks that they neglect the long-term evaluation needs.

The advantages and disadvantages of an inside, "second-party" evaluator are similar to those just described. This approach means the program coordinator will lose some direct contact with the information. However, this loss can be offset by the advantage of having an evaluator serve as a mentor to the coordinator. In this situation, the evaluator should serve only in an advisory capacity.

Using an outside, "third-party" evaluator provides the greatest likelihood of obtaining objective information on the staff development program. However, the trade-off for this objectivity is that the outside evaluator typically is a part-time consultant who has other full-time commitments. Differing levels of commitment to the program for the program coordinator and program evaluator can cause misunderstandings and conflict.

The external program evaluator is a middle person who must be able to negotiate with program managers and determine the audience for an evaluation.

Skills of Internal Evaluator

The internal evaluator typically has multiple roles. Occasionally a program will employ a full-time evaluator who is expected to have skills similar to those described in the next section for the external evaluator.

The internal evaluator is responsible for gathering information on district, school, and staff needs as well as program participation and program effectiveness. For these tasks, the program evaluator should have the following minimum skills:

1. Writing and speaking abilities.
2. The ability to use descriptive statistics and comparative statistics through at least the t-test.
3. Background in participant observation and interviewing.
4. Background in survey development and administration.

Additional helpful skills would be familarity with the basic evaluation models, ability to use microcomputers for word processing and data analysis, and background in tests and measurements.

Any program that depends solely on internal evaluation, whether by the program coordinator or another staff member, should occasionally seek the advice of an external evaluator. This contact could range from a single meeting where the program evaluation procedures used are reviewed to an extensive audit of the procedures and information obtained. The goals of such a review would be evaluation objectivity and integrity.

Skills of External Evaluator

Independent program evaluators will bring to a program observation and data handling skills. The amount of expertise that evaluators should have in the program area to be evaluated is an unresolved question. Too much content expertise can bias the evaluation by causing evaluators to reject all possible alternatives except the ones to which they subscribe; too little content expertise can result in evaluators missing important, subtle aspects of a program.

The external program evaluator is a middle person who must be able to negotiate with program managers and determine the audience for an evaluation. In addition, the evaluator often must develop criteria for judgment, design the evaluation, identify sources of data or instruments for data collection, supervise the administration of the instruments, assimilate and analyze the data, and present the results. Data collection may involve on-site observation and unstructured interviews, document review, testing, or survey administration. With these tasks in mind, the program coordinator who uses an external evaluator should look for an educational researcher with the following skills:

1. Group processing abilities.
2. Writing and speaking abilities.
3. Basic statistical knowledge through at least factorial design and multiple linear regression analysis.
4. Basic background in measurement, survey development, and instrument construction and administration.
5. Basic computer knowledge, including use of major statistical packages such as SAS or SPSS. (Currently there are several good packages for microcomputers that might be acceptable such as MINITAB).
6. Grounding in ethnographic procedures, including skills in participant observation, interviewing, developing field notes, and analysis of qualitative data.
7. Ability to separate oneself from project management so as to serve as an independent advisor to the program.

Roles Of Evaluators

There is no single role for the program evaluator. Roles can vary from the program advocate in the quasi-legal model to the reporter in the behavioral objectives model to the commentator in the systems and case study models. The staff development program coordinator needs to determine the role needed before beginning a program evaluation. The role will depend on the audience to be served by the evaluation.

One needs to remember that the two main reasons for an evaluation to be used are (1) political concerns and (2) whether the evaluation was built into the program with the intention of being used. (Patton, 1982). As has been illustrated in the Schenley High Teachers' Center (Denion & LeMahieu, 1985), program evaluation can be integral to program development through mentor relationships with program leaders, if the feedback is actually valued and desired.

Evaluation Recommendations

An ongoing part of any staff development program should be evaluation. Either an internal or external evaluator should use goal-based or systems monitoring procedures. If an outside evaluator is not part of the ongoing evaluation, it would be prudent to occasionally hire one to provide formative feedback through a case study evaluation. It is likely that this outside evaluator will verify and document what the project coordinator and staff already know. However, this approach also can provide a fresh look at institutionalized procedures — a look that can lead to significant program changes and improvements.

The quasi-legal evaluation model should be used if the program coordinator needs to defend the staff development program before a school board, funding agency, or other adversarial group. Frequently, the need for this type of defense is known a year or two in advance. If this is the case, the early employment of an evaluator experienced in quasi-legal presentation is recommended.

Assuming that the main purpose of an evaluation is to provide program staff with planning information and that secondary audiences would include district administrators, the school board, and professional staff, the following questions could serve as the focus for evaluation:

1. Were the broad objectives of the staff development program met?
2. Were the specific objectives of the staff development activities met?
3. Did participants benefit from the specific staff development activity? Examples of benefits could be knowledge, skills, attitudes, or stess reduction.
4. Did skill- or knowledge-oriented staff development activities result in participants increasing the frequency and rigor with which the recommended practices were used?
5. How many teachers (and/or administrators) participated in staff development activities?
6. How many schools participated in staff development activities?
7. Did the students of teachers participating in staff development activities benefit from teacher participation?
8. Did the teachers in schools where principals participated in staff development activities benefit from principal participation?

Evaluation activities that might be used to monitor a staff development program are:

1. *Broad Objectives* - Analysis and summarize staff development activity information.
2. *Specific Activity Objectives* - These can be assessed from several vantage points depending upon how program objectives are written. The three most common procedures are:
   a. At the end of a staff development activity, have participants rate the degree to which each activity objective was met.
   b. A few weeks after a staff development activity, have supervisors of the participants rate the frequency with which the behaviors specified in the objectives have been observed.
   c. Directly test (or observe) for the behavior specified in the activity objectives.
3. *Gain* - Assess through direct testing (or observation) using a pretest - posttest model. The participants would be tested on the expected behavior before and after the activity to look for change. Frequently, a control (non-participating) group is used to make sure that any observed gains are due to the activity.
4. *Use of Skills* - Assess through survey or direct observation. A few weeks after the staff development activity, staff are surveyed (or observed/interviewed) to determine the degree to which the "new" skills or knowledge have been implemented. As in 3, frequently a control group is used to make sure that implementation is a result of the activity.

5. *Participation* - Count the numbers of staff members who have participated in staff development activities. Count both total participation and the number of different staff members that have participated. For example, during a year, 200 staff members may have participated in staff development activities, representing 75 different individuals. These numbers are referred to as duplicated and unduplicated counts, respectively.

6. *Schools* - Count duplicated and unduplicated participation by schools.

7. *Students* - Many activities will be directed toward increasing teachers' skills in instruction or knowledge of content. For some of these activities, it will be assumed that the activity should result in increased student learning. Assess this through direct student testing using a pretest - posttest model. Typically, a control group of matched students is used in the comparison.

8. *Principals* - Some activities may be directed toward changing principals' skills. Assess results of this type of activity by surveying teachers to determine whether or not there have been any observable changes in principals' behaviors. This usually is done using a pretest - posttest model.

Remember that staff development program evaluation must fit into the collegial planning and implementation of the program as well as report on the value of the program to both staff and students. A goal-based evaluation focusing on questions like those listed above will meet these criteria. Once program goals are specified and evaluation strategies determined, the program evaluation can be systematically implemented. The result will be needed information for staff and others to use in planning and in evaluating results.

Figure 7.3
Assessing Your Program: Staff Development Program Outcome Evaluation Checklist

This checklist can be used to assess your own program evaluation. It has been adapted from a scale presented at the 1987 annual NSDC meeting (Hales, 1987).

Program Element	Evaluation Activity	Check
Audience(s)	Has the audience for the evaluation been identified?	[ ] Yes [ ] No
	specify who	
Evaluator	Has the evaluator been identified?	[ ] Yes [ ] No
	specify who	
	Who are the obligations of evaluator to: employer, program staff, etc?	
	What are the constraints on the evaluator? Program?	
	Is the evaluator independent?	

(Fig. 7.3, cont.)			
	Is evaluator reporter? Mediator? Commentator?		
Objectives	Are there program objectives?	[ ] Yes	
	If yes, list. If no, why?	[ ] No	
	Are objectives explicitly stated and measurable?	[ ] Yes	
		[ ] No	
	Are there implicit objectives?	[ ] Yes	
	If yes, what are they?	[ ] No	
	Is there a consensus on objectives among constituents?	[ ] Yes	
		[ ] No	
	If no, is mediation expected?	[ ] Yes	
		[ ] No	
	If no, whose objectives are to be used? _____		
		[ ] No	
	Are objectives linked to specific program activities?	[ ] Yes	
		[ ] No	
	If no, can they be linked?	[ ] Yes	
	If yes, how?	[ ] No	
	Are there program objectives for:		
	Program Staff	[ ] Yes	
		[ ] No	
	Teachers	[ ] Yes	
		[ ] No	
	Administrators	[ ] Yes	
		[ ] No	
	Students	[ ] Yes	
		[ ] No	
	Others _____	[ ] Yes	
		[ ] No	
Standards	Are there explicit criteria specified for judging outcomes?	[ ] Yes	
		[ ] No	
	Who determined the criteria? _____		
	How were the criteria selected? _____		
	Is there consensus among constituents?	[ ] Yes	
		[ ] No	
	If no, is mediation expected?	[ ] Yes	
		[ ] No	

If no, whose criteria will be used? _____

Are standards measurable?　　　　　　　　　　[　] Yes
　　　　　　　　　　　　　　　　　　　　　　　[　] No

Have standards been met?　　　　　　　　　　　[　] Yes
　　　　　　　　　　　　　　　　　　　　　　　[　] No

Design　　Are the following elements in the design:

Budget　　　　　　　　　　　　　　　　　　　[　] Yes
　　　　　　　　　　　　　　　　　　　　　　　[　] No

Constraints _____　[　] Yes
　　　　　　　　　　　　　　　　　　　　　　　[　] No

Program Components _____　　[　] Yes
　　　　　　　　　　　　　　　　　　　　　　　[　] No

Processes & Procedures　　　　　　　　　　　　[　] Yes
　　　　　　　　　　　　　　　　　　　　　　　[　] No

Contextual Variables　　　　　　　　　　　　　[　] Yes
　　　　　　　　　　　　　　　　　　　　　　　[　] No

Objectives & Outcomes　　　　　　　　　　　　[　] Yes
　　　　　　　　　　　　　　　　　　　　　　　[　] No

Types of Design to be used:

Descriptive　　　　　　　　　　　　　　　　　[　] Yes
　　　　　　　　　　　　　　　　　　　　　　　[　] No

Pretest-Posttest　　　　　　　　　　　　　　　[　] Yes
　　　　　　　　　　　　　　　　　　　　　　　[　] No

Posttest Only with Control　　　　　　　　　　[　] Yes
　　　　　　　　　　　　　　　　　　　　　　　[　] No

Pretest-Posttest with Control　　　　　　　　　[　] Yes
　　　　　　　　　　　　　　　　　　　　　　　[　] No

Other _____　[　] Yes
　　　　　　　　　　　　　　　　　　　　　　　[　] No

Are instruments appropriate?　　　　　　　　　[　] Yes
　　　　　　　　　　　　　　　　　　　　　　　[　] No

Are data collection procedures appropriate?　　[　] Yes
　　　　　　　　　　　　　　　　　　　　　　　[　] No

Are data analysis procedures appropriate?　　　[　] Yes
　　　　　　　　　　　　　　　　　　　　　　　[　] No

Are procedures for reporting appropriate?　　　[　] Yes
　　　　　　　　　　　　　　　　　　　　　　　[　] No

References

Alkins, M.C., Daillak, R., & White, R. (1979). *Using evaluations: Does it make a difference?* Beverly Hills, CA: Sage Publications.

Apple, M.W. (1974). The process and ideology of valuing in educational settings. In Apple, M.W., Subkoviak, M.J., and Lufler, H.S., Jr. (Eds.) *Educational evaluation: Analysis and responsibility.* Berkley, CA: McCutchan Publishing Corporation.

Cooley, W.W., & Bickel, W.E. (1986). *Decision-oriented educational research.* Norwell, MA: Kluwer Academic Publishers.

Cooley, W.W., & Lohnes, P.R. (1976). *Evaluation research in education.* New York: John Wiley and Sons.

Denton, S.E., & LeMahieu, P.G. (1985, August). Evaluation research as an integral part of Pittsburgh's in-service staff development center. *Evaluation News, 6*(3).

Doctors, S.I., & Wokutch, R.E. (1980). Social program evaluation: Six models. In Perloff, R. and Perloff, E. (Eds.) *Values, ethics and standards in evaluation.* San Francisco, CA: Jossey-Bass.

Fullan, M. (1982). *The meaning of educational change.* New York: Teachers College Press, Columbia University.

Hales, L.W. (1987, December). Evaluation checklist. In Marshall, J.C., & L.W. Hales, *Staff development program evaluation.* Symposium present at the annual meeting of the National Staff Development Council, Seattle, WA.

Hales, L.W. (1986, April). *Reporting, judging and other gods.* Paper presented at the annual meeting of the American Educational Research Association, San Francisco, CA.

Hales, L.W. (1987, December). Summative evaluation. Presented in J.C. Marshall & L.W. Hales, *Evaluation models for staff development.* Concurrent session presented at the annual meeting of the National Staff Development Conference, Seattle, WA.

House, E.R. (1981). *Evaluating with validity.* Beverly Hills, CA: Sage Publications.

Hovey, S. (1986, Fall). Teachers at the center. *American Educator,* 26-30.

Johnson, J.A., & Brant, J.B. (1986, December). *Using research to monitor and tailor staff development.* Symposium presented at the annual meeting of the National Staff Development Council, Atlanta, GA.

Little, J.W. (1982). Making sure: Contributions and requirements of good evaluation. *Journal of Staff Development, 3*(1), 25-47.

Marshall, J.C. (1988). *Staff development program evaluation using Stake's contingency and congruence model: A writing program example.* Unpublished manuscript, North Carolina State University, Raleigh, NC.

Marshall, J.C., & Caldwell, S.D. (1982). Information management and evaluation in staff development: A case report. *Journal of Staff Development, 3*(1), 84-101.

McLaughlin, M.W. (1975). *Evaluation and reform.* Cambridge, MA: Ballinger.

Owens, T.R. (1973). Educational evaluation by adversary proceeding. In House, E.R. (Ed.) *School evaluation.* Berkeley, CA: McCutchan Publishing Corporation.

Patton, M.Q. (1982). Refelections on evaluating staff development: The view from the iron cow. *Journal of Staff Development, 3*(1), 6-25.

Pritchard, R.J., & Marshall, J.C. (1987, April). *Impact on classroom practices and student achievement of second generation teacher training in a writing program: Implications for staff development.* Paper presented at the annual meeting of the American Educational Research Association, Washington, DC.

Rossi, P.H., Freedman, H.E., & Wright, S.R. (1979). *Evaluation: A systematic approach.* Beverly Hills, CA: Sage Publications.

Ryan, T.F., & Crowell, R.A. (1982). Evaluation for non evaluators: Assessing staff development. *Journal of Staff Development, 3*(1), 156-169.

Shapiro, J.Z. (1985). Evaluation of a worksite program in health science and medicine: An application of Sake's model of contingency and congruence. *Educational Evaluation and Policy Analysis, 7*(1), 47-56.

Simmons, J.M. (1982). Fighting the budget battle with evidence: Cost effectiveness, data-based decision-making. *Journal of Staff Development, 3*(1), 118-146.

Stake, R.E. (1967). The countenance of educational evaluation. *Teachers College Record, 68,* 523-540.

Stake, R.E. (1973). Measuring what learners learn. In House, E.R. (ed.) *School evaluation.* Berkely, CA: McCutchan.

Stake, R.E. (1976). The countenance of educational evaluation. In C. Weis (Ed.), *Evaluating action programs.* Boston, MA: Allyn and Bacon.

Wolf, R.L. (1975, November). Trial by jury: The process. *Phi Delta Kappan, 57,* 185-187.

Wood, F.H., Caldwell, S.D., & Thompson, S.R. (1986). Practical realities for school-based staff development. *Journal of Staff Development, 7*(1), 52-66.

Worthen, B.R., & Sanders, J.R. (1973). *Educational evaluation: Theory and Practice.* Worthington, OH: Charles A. Jones.

Staff development program evaluation must fit into the collegial planning and implementation of the program as well as report on the value of the program to both staff and students.

Chapter 8

Managing Change: An Integrated Part of Staff Development

Susan Loucks-Horsley

One of the many roles of a staff developer is to create the right set of conditions to enable change to occur.

Staff development and change go hand-in-hand, since the intention of staff development is to change behaviors, attitudes, and skills. One of the many roles of a staff developer is to create the right set of conditions to enable change to occur.

Although this sounds logical, change has mystified many and stymied even more in their pursuit of school and classroom improvements. We have a morgue full of failures: new programs whose artifacts cram our shelves and closets; catalogs of staff development offerings that barely caused a "blip" on the screen; and a large number of teachers whose response to new staff development efforts is, "not that again — they tried that ten years ago!"

Change takes time and attention. It is simultaneously a highly personal experience and one that is tangled in the structures, norms, and idiosyncrasies of the organizations, the schools, and districts, in which teaching and learning occur. Whether change occurs depends on a myriad of factors — so many that one might attribute the success of a given staff development effort, at worst, to a favorable alignment of the stars or, at best, to the artistry of a particular staff developer.

Although art has its place in the change process, there is also a large amount of science to call on for help. The number of studies of change in schools far outweighs studies of such phenomena as effective schools. Studies of change have helped those responsible for designing and implementing staff development programs that seek to make immediate and enduring changes.

In this chapter we draw on this knowledge of the change process to describe key dimensions of interest to staff developers who are serious about their roles in managing change. The four "P's" — people, processes, practices, and policies — are critical to the success of change efforts. These critical ingredients must be considered in every effort aimed at change if it is to succeed.

* People — their needs, motivations, behaviors, and the roles they play in change.
* Processes — how change progresses over time and what can be done along the way to ensure its success.
* Practices — characteristics of the innovation being introduced.
* Policies — the pressure or push from policy makers and administrators that takes the form of mandates, guidelines, regulations, expectations, and direction.

We know a great deal about each of these dimensions of change and how they support or hinder the process. But it is the art of managing change that is the staff developer's challenge. Like artist Alexander Calder who uses scientific data about materials, balance, and air currents to create mobiles, staff developers must artfully combine knowledge from research on change to help educators make schools better places for students.

People in the Process of Change

Getting a handle on how people change and how to help them interests staff developers and researchers alike. Fortunately, this is the area of research on change that has made, perhaps, the greatest contribution.

One research-based model for individual change that staff developers have used extensively is the Concerns-Based Adoption Model (CBAM) (Hord, Rutherford, Huling-Austin, & Hall, 1987). Figure 8.1 illustrates one dimension of the model: Stages of Concern. These stages represent a gradual progression by an individual engaged in change from concerns about self (What is it and what will it mean for me?) through concerns about task (Why is it taking so much time and effort, and will I ever get organized?) to concerns about impact (Are students benefiting, and what can I do to better meet their needs?).

Figure 8.1
Stages of Concern: Typical Expressions of Concern
About the Innovation

Stages of Concern	Expressions of Concern
6 Refocusing	I have an idea about something that would work even better.
5 Collaboration	I am concerned about relating what I am doing with what other instructors are doing.
4 Consequence	How is my use affecting kids?
3 Management	I seem to be spending all my time in getting material ready.
2 Personal	How will using it affect me?
1 Informational	I would like to know more about it.
0 Awareness	I am not concerned about it (the innovation).

From Hall, G.E., & Loucks, S.F. (1978). Teacher concerns as a basis for facilitating staff development. *Teachers College Record, 80*(1), 36-53.

Stages of concern are developmental (Hall & Loucks, 1978), a fact that has many implications for staff developers. First, change takes time. People need to work through their lower-stage concerns before higher stages can emerge. It is likely to take three to five years for change to reach the stage of teacher concern for the needs of students. Second, personal concerns are a normal part of change. People need help resolving these concerns, not criticism for having them. Finally, the stages give us endless clues for designing staff development efforts that respond appropriately over time to the kinds of concerns that emerge.

A number of researchers have focused on what helps people as they undergo change (Crandall & Loucks, 1983; Fullan, 1982; Loucks-Horsley & Hergert, 1985; McLaughlin & Marsh, 1978). Some of the findings can be organized in three phases of change: initiation, implementation, and institutionalization.

Initiation

During the initiation phase, people have informational and personal concerns. Teachers need to know what the change is and how it works; what it looks like in classrooms; what materials, rearrangements, and time will be required to do it; what workshops, release time, and other support they will get; and what priority it has with the principal, central office staff members, and parents. Sometimes teachers either make or participate in making the choice of what they will do. Such participation sometimes lessens the intensity of concerns, but teachers still need answers to their basic questions.

Developing a clear image of what will be implemented and what it will mean to the individual is an important task for the staff developer. This image can be sharpened through brief awareness or overview sessions, videotapes, and focused classroom visits. Involving the principal and other key administrators and having them send clear messages of commitment and support is important. Engaging staff members in discussions of how they will implement the change, what shape it might take in the classroom or school, and what they need for support during the process helps develop commitment early, regardless of whether staff members actually participated in the decision to make the change.

Like the excellent companies described by Peters and Waterman (1982), schools and districts engaged in successful staff development efforts have a penchant for action. They do not dally at the initiation phase. Too much "wind up" often leaves people without the energy or motivation to actually do anything, yet the extended needs assessment and planning processes that some staff developers use subvert quick action. A successful solution is to use some of the initiation activities described above, convincing teachers to suspend disbelief long enough to try something (Crandall, 1983). With good training from staff developers, encouragement and support from administrators, and the agreement that all will work together to solve problems that arise, implementation can proceed.

Implementation

It seems that we finally have given up the belief that one-shot, hit-and-run workshops are the key to lasting change in education. While the implementation phase begins with focused training in new skills and behaviors, it continues with many support and follow-up activities designed to "debug" teachers' use of the new practice and to encourage them to persist through the usually choppy first few months.

During the implementation phase, the predominant concern is management, although some information and personal concerns remain. The questions, "How do I do it?" and "How do I do it without going crazy?" haunt new users and, thus, staff developers.

Initial training provides teachers with hands-on experience with the materials and strategies they will use with their students, allowing them to practice in a safe, supportive environment. Along with training, coaching in classrooms assures teachers that they are making the right moves. Follow-up visits and group discussions help teachers solve problems and let them discover that they are not alone in their concerns. These activities maintain commitment and bolster collegiality. As teachers become more comfortable with new behaviors, they can use these sessions as a rich source of ideas related to the new practice. Such sessions also keep teachers from being distracted by competing demands.

People need to work through their lower-stage concerns before higher stages can emerge. It is likely to take three to five years for change to reach the stage of teacher concern for the needs of students.

Institutionalization

Most people working toward change congratulate themselves if they get through the first year or two successfully. By then, teachers' management concerns have all but disappeared, and some concerns about impact are emerging. But celebration can be premature. After the excitement of implementation, people often lose interest; the change fades from view and from use. In other instances, a change effort can be strong one year and gone the next, due largely to the elimination of support or the disappearance of a key person. Fortunately, both of these scenarios can be avoided with some advance planning (Miles, 1983).

The role of a champion or advocate is crucial at the front end of change efforts; sometimes this is the role of a staff developer. But often the person in this role thrives on start-up activities and loses interest as implementation becomes routine, or is recognized as a "star" and offered a position or opportunity that can't be refused. It is important to think ahead about a replacement for the advocate — usually more of a manager — or about dividing up the functions that the advocate played early in the process. These actions increase chances that continuing the new program won't depend on one individual.

Integrating a new practice into the structure, systems, and routines of a school or district enhances the probability that the practice will remain. Integration involves creating a line item in the budget for necessary staff, equipment, and materials. It also requires writing the practice into curriculum guidelines, routinely ordering consumable materials, and orienting and training new or reassigned staff members. Add to these activities, which can be the responsibility of a staff developer, regular encouragement and public recognition of the practice by administrators, and the possibility that a new program will become institutionalized is increased.

Schools and districts engaged in successful staff development efforts have a penchant for action.

Supporting People in the Process of Change

Attention to all three phases of the change process is a lot of work that clearly can't be done by staff developers alone. It is often more useful to identify the many activities and functions that need to be carried out and then to look for the person who is in the best position to do each. In change, there are roles for everybody, from teachers to policy makers.

Interestingly, a central office coordinator or consultant — often a staff developer — is apt to become a key player in the change process. Few early studies identified central office personnel as important, and most budget makers consider them to be nonessential. But several studies (Loucks-Horsley & Cox, 1984; Hall et al., 1983; McLaughlin & Marsh, 1978) indicate that a central office person can be in the best position to scan the environment for effective new practices, build commitment among school staff members, arrange for teacher training or actually train teachers, help teachers plan for implementation in their own classrooms, and troubleshoot teachers' problems and concerns during the first year of use. Further, central office people have the ability to observe many classrooms and find appropriate people to link together, both to share common problems and to match problems with solutions. They often have the resources, the expertise, and sometimes the clout to make sure instructional or curricular changes occur.

Principals have their roles, too, although many teachers have managed to improve their teaching despite an inactive principal. (When principals actively work against an effort in a school, however, the effort has little chance of success.) In a best-case scenario, principals have the important role of setting and clarifying expectations either for or, even better, with staff members, monitoring progress during implementation, and attending to teacher concerns so that help is provided when needed.

Principals and other administrators have the additional leadership role of providing a little push to teachers when their enthusiasm lags or when they need help clarifying their priorities. "Forceful leadership" is provided by administrators who initiate as well as support their staff members in significantly changing their teaching. Such leadership is found in many successful improvement efforts.

Finally, external consultants or trainers provide teachers with skills and tools they need to implement a new practice. Although earlier researchers (Berman & McLaughlin, 1975) found that external help did not contribute to improvement, the types of people they found giving it were those with a theoretical bent who had little contact with the reality of the classroom and no particular responsibility for the ongoing implementation of a new practice.

Along with training, coaching in classrooms assures teachers that they are making the right moves.

In more recent studies, external help came from teachers-turned-trainers, from individuals who had actually developed a new practice, or from those who had spent a lot of time using it. Such trainers know precisely what to expect when using a practice and can swap war stories with other teachers; moreover, they have the kind of credibility needed to convince teachers to suspend disbelief and try something new (Crandall, 1983). This new breed of trainer or consultant also knows the value of coaching and follow-up assistance, and is either on hand to provide both or helps school or district people design a system to do so.

None of these findings negates the role teachers must play in change. Teachers' actions and behaviors determine whether learning will indeed improve. But teachers need a great deal of support — both materially and psychologically — if they are to change what they do in their classrooms.

New Practices and Their Role in Change

Staff developers are increasingly aware that change for the sake of change is worthless, and that what is chosen to be implemented is integral to whether or not improvement goals are achieved.

Schools succeed when the new practices they select or develop are:

* *Well-defined.* It is possible to describe, talk about, and observe the most important teacher and student behaviors, instructional materials and strategies, and management systems and structures that constitute the practices.

* *Effective.* The practices have been tried and found to produce appropriate results with enough teachers and students to be believable. A statistical evaluation is not essential, but an opinion or testimonial from a lone teacher who has used a practice is not enough. We've foisted too many untested and ultimately useless practices on teachers in the past to dare to continue to do it.

* *"Classroom friendly."* These practices are not undigested, untransformed research results like "time on task;" general descriptions of optimal states of affairs like equal access, participation, or high achievement; or simply materials or equipment like microcomputers. The practices are designed in such a way that teachers can immediately use them in their classrooms (Loucks & Zacchei, 1983).

Integrating a new practice into the structure, systems, and routines of a school or district enhances the probability that the practice will remain.

Many schools that have chosen to develop their own practices have incorporated these characteristics in them. In addition, and contrary to conventional wisdom, researchers have found that practices and programs developed in one setting can be used in the same way and with similar success in other places (Crandall & Loucks, 1983; Emrick, et al., 1977). As we learn how to locate, evaluate, and disseminate practices designed for schools, we are finding that transfer is not only possible but cost-effective. Adopting a practice is about one-tenth as costly as developing one. Pools of practices exist in many states as well as through the National Diffusion Network, which disseminates more than 300 programs in all content areas.

Managing change means knowing where to go to learn about proven practices, programs, and processes; how to assess features of new practices and match them to the philosophy, style, student population, and resources of a particular school or district; and how to clearly define what the core components of a new practice are so that adaptations will not destroy the hoped-for results (Loucks-Horsley & Hergert, 1985). A new practice has greater potential for lasting change when all those procedures are followed.

How Mandates Contribute to Change

There has been considerable debate over the years about the influence of mandates on school and classroom improvement. We all want to buy into the image of the self-improving professional who always is looking for and adopting new, improved ways of teaching. We want to believe that change occurs because people want to do their jobs better, not because someone else says to change.

Yet for many reasons, this image is false. Teachers are targets of competing demands, both in school and out; rewards for change are few and far between. Just meeting current demands is becoming increasingly difficult, and searching out and implementing change takes time and other resources. Furthermore, change is not a "natural act" — maintaining the status quo is.

Thus, when teachers engage in deliberate change, it is often in response to a mandate from the principal, district, school board, or state. Mandates have proven to be critical for some interesting resource. Staff developers, of course, would prefer that teachers make a change because they agree with it, not simply because the change is mandated. Often, however, they are in a position that requires helping teachers adopt new behaviors before the teachers themselves have chosen to do so.

Fortunately, research on change indicates that change in attitudes does *not* always have to occur before behaviors can change. In his synthesis of current research, Guskey (1986) refutes the conventional wisdom that attitude change must precede behavior change by

---

Principals have the important role of setting and clarifying expectations either for or, even better, with staff members, monitoring progress and attending to teacher concerns.

---

starting with two "givens:" (a) the greatest reward for teachers is the learning of their students and (b) there are a great many practices that are known to enhance student learning. He then argues, as the research confirms, that teachers who master new, proven practices, even if they have not chosen to do so, will be convinced of the practices' value when their students' learning improves. This change in attitude, the commitment to continue use of a practice, is far deepeer and more firmly held than the "ownership" many seek to develop before a practice is even tried out (Crandall & Loucks, 1983).

This is not an argument to force everyone to do things they don't want to do. Research does, however, support staff developers who have to live with mandates all the time; who believe in some standardization of practice within and across schools; who face teachers who will never change their minds first about something new, regardless of what it is; and who don't have time or resources to convince everyone ahead of time that change is a good thing.

It is pointless to debate whether attitudes need to change before behaviors. As Fullan (1982) notes, the most succesful chang is simultaneously top-down and bottom-up. The best strategy is to work both sides of the fence. Help people develop commitment ahead of time by providing them with all possible information, incentives, and opportunities for input. Be sure that the change is one that will, in fact, benefit students if used well. Then get going, which may mean convincing some to suspend disbelief and try it while pressuring others to participate whether they like it or not. (The latter may be delayed until others have tried it and liked it, thus convincing some of the hold-outs to participate.) Provide all the training and support needed to help the reluctant ones change their behaviors. Finally, identify and celebrate successes experienced by both teachers and students.

Using policies made by others to advantage is part of the art of managing change. With supportive policies, effective practices, keen attention to the ways people experience change, and strategies to support change in the short term as well as the long haul, staff developers can manage change effectively.

None of these recommendations can ensure that a change will outlive a teacher strike, a new superintendent or principal, or a major budget cut. Yet they can go a long way toward weaving the change firmly into the fabric of the school and classroom and toward fending off the threats to change experienced daily by everyone in education.

Figure 8.2
Assessing Your Program

In your staff development efforts, do you:

1. Assess, either formally or informally, the concerns of participants and make every effort to address them?
2. Plan the delivery of staff development according to how participants' concerns will progress and adjust your efforts along the way?
3. Create realistic expectations and then plan for an adequate amount of time for staff development to result in the kinds of change desired (i.e., three to five years for significant changes)?
4. Address information and personnel concerns early, creating a clear image of what participants will be doing and the support they will receive? Do you engage them in discussions and decisions when possible?
5. Provide ongoing, rather than one-shot, training that includes opportunities for practice and individual help to refine the program in their classrooms?
6. Provide support and encouragement after implementation, ensuring that leadership is maintained, a line item is in the budget, the program is part of the mission, curriculum or contracted responsibility of staff, and new teachers are routinely trained?
7. Identify important leadership and support functions that need to be played at building and district level, and engage the most appropriate people to orchestrate their efforts?
8. Choose, help others choose, or develop well-defined, effective, classroom friendly programs or practices for your staff development offerings?
9. Work to turn mandates and requirements into opportunities to help people try out new skills and practices? Do you call upon the clout of administrators to convince those reluctant to change to suspend disbelief and try?
10. Work closely with teachers, administrators, and others to select staff development offerings wisely and provide all the help and support needed for individuals to implement changes successfully?
11. Restrict the number of change efforts progress at any one point in time? Do you set priorities and stick to them?
12. View staff development as a vehicle for change? Are you clear about what the changes should be and how to recognize them. Do you monitor and adjust the effort continually to reach the goal?

Figure 8.3
Competencies

In order to implement the ideas in this chapter, staff developers should:

1. Know the major factors contributing to successful change and how they look in practice.
2. Know the major components of the Concerns-Based Adoption Model and how to assess Stages of Concern, either formally or informally.
3. Know how to define a practice in such a way that people can identify how it looks when it is being implemented well.
4. Know how to work with cross-role groups in planning, problem solving, and decision making.
5. Know the facets of planning, monitoring, and adjusting plans.
6. Know how to select and train good support people, (i.e.,teachers who provide help, advice, and even training to other teachers).
7. Know the components of good training.
8. Know how to recognize success, encourage people, and establish commitment.
9. Know how to manage people, tasks, and time and how to help others do so.
10. Know how to convince people to do something (i.e., give them support, try a new practice, reallocate their time or resources).

External help came from teachers-turned-trainers, from individuals who had actually developed a new practice, or from those who had spent a lot of time using it.

References

Crandall, D.P., & Loucks, S.F. (1983). *People, policies, and practices: Examining the chain of school improvement. Vol. X: A Roadmap for School Improvement.* Andover, MA: The NETWORK, Inc.

Crandall, D.P. (1983). The teacher's role in school improvement. *Educational Leadership, 41*(3), 6-9.

Emrick, J., Peterson, S., & Agarwala-Rogers, R. (1977). *Evaluation of the national diffusion network.* Menlo Park, CA: Stanford Research Institute.

Fullan, M. (1982). *The meaning of educational change.* Toronto: Ontario Institute for the Study of Education (OISE) Press.

Guskey, T.R. (1986) Staff development and the process of teacher change. *Educational Researcher, 15*(5), 5-12.

Hall, G., & Loucks, S. (1978). Teacher concerns as a basis for facilitating and personalizing staff development. *Teachers College Record, 80*(1), 36-53.

Hord, S.M., Hall, G.E., & Stiegelbauer, S.M. (1983, April). *Principals don't do it alone: The role of the consigliere.* Paper presented at the American Educational Research Association Annual Meeting, Montreal.

Hord, S.M., Rutherford, W.L., Huling-Austin, L., & Hall, G.E. (1987). *Taking charge of change.* Alexandria, VA: Association for Supervision and Curriculum Development.

Loucks-Horsley, S., & Cox, P.L. (1985). What the national commission and studies of education overlooked: The "how" of school change. *Journal of Staff Development, 5*(2), 21-28.

Loucks-Horsley, S., & Hergert, L.F. (1985). *An action guide to school improvement.* Alexandria, VA: Association for Supervision and Curriculum Development.

Loucks, S.F., & Zacchei, D.A. (1983). Applying our findings to today's innovations. *Educational Leadership, 41*(3), 28-31.

McLaughlin, M.W., & Marsh, D.D. (1978). Staff development and school change. *Teachers College of Record, 80*(1), 69-94.

Miles, M.B. (1983). Unraveling the mysteries of institutionalization. *Educational Leadership, 41*(3), 14-22.

Peters, T.J., & Waterman, R.H., Jr. (1982). *In search of excellence.* New York: Harper & Row.

The practices have been tried and found to produce appropriate results with enough teachers and students to be believable.

Chapter 9

Inquiry-Oriented Staff Development: Using Research as a Source of Tools, Not Rules

Using research only as a source of prescriptions does not help participants in staff development activities become enlightened decision makers.

Georgea Mohlman Sparks
and
Joanne M. Simmons

Using research only as a source of findings and prescriptions does not meet one of the most important goals of staff development — to help participants become enlightened decision makers. Educators should not go about blindly doing what research says. Rather, research processes and findings should be used as conceptual tools to enlighten decision making.

Two Uses Of Research In Staff Development

A concrete example illustrates two very different uses of research. Joe went to a workshop where he heard about research on wait time (Rowe, 1974). He went back to his classroom and diligently practiced waiting three seconds after asking every question. He found there were times — quick drill on math facts, for example — when the technique seemed to slow the class pace, and he began to have some management problems during those periods. But he persisted in the use of wait time because "research said it worked."

George, on the other hand, learned about wait time in a very different setting. During a workshop, he read a brief summary of the research, discussed when the technique would work best and when it would not work, and designed a plan to systematically experiment with wait time in his class. As he tried the strategy under several conditions, he found it worked well for complex thinking questions, but not as well for those facts he wanted students to be able to recall automatically.

George noted that many of his slower learners were still having unsuccessful responses to complex thinking types of questions and asked a colleague to record his wait time with these students. He found that he was not waiting long enough with them, so he extended the wait to five seconds. As he tinkered with the technique, he developed a deeper understanding of wait time. He made the technique his own rather than blindly following research.

Too often, staff developers present only the findings from research without striving for a deeper understanding of how and why the research was done, what the sample was, and in what context it was conducted. Traditionally, we have thought our job was merely to get teachers to use research-based practices in their classes. Joyce and Showers (1983) call this "horizontal transfer," the ability to use a technique "on call." But it is clear that there is much more to good teaching than just using a particular strategy *accurately*. The teacher must use the strategy *appropriately*. Joyce and Showers call this "vertical transfer." It involves knowing when and with whom it is best to use the new technique. This reflective, inquiry-oriented, decision-making aspect of teaching has been given too little emphasis in staff development programs (Simmons & Sparks, 1985).

Currently, there is considerable support for promoting teacher inquiry. Teachers' thinking has been the focus of much research (Clark & Peterson, 1986). Hunter (1985) has emphasized teacher decision making and decried the use of her concepts as recipes for teachers to follow blindly. Other experts (Schon, 1983, 1978; Simmons & Schuette, 1988) say teacher education needs to develop teachers who are equipped and willing to reflectively inquire into the teaching and learning process. If this is the goal of professional development for educators — and we think it must be — then staff development needs to become much more than showing practitioners how to use prescribed research-based skills.

History of Using Research in Practice

The past 20 years have been marked by a dramatic increase in our knowledge of effective teaching, learning, and schooling. These variables, theoretical models, questions, data-collection techniques, and findings have revolutionized how we view teaching, learning, supervision, leadership, and teacher education.

Early studies of teachers focused primarily on links between variables such as teacher experience or personality and outcomes such as student learning. This research viewed the teacher as an effective person(ality). For example, it seemed reasonable that teacher warmth and preparation would enhance student learning, but little evidence was found to support this view (Ryans, 1960).

During the 1960s and 1970s, researchers investigated the links between classroom processes (i.e., brisk pacing, teacher questions, and reinforcement) and outcomes such as student test scores. This process-product research treated the teacher as a skilled performer. Unfortunately, many staff developers and evaluators have perpetuated this view by prescribing all-purpose, effective teaching behaviors for teachers. In many cases, this use of research has resulted in teachers resisting a view of teaching they see as overly simplistic.

As more effective teaching research findings were published, it became apparent that some results conflicted. For example, Kounin (1970) emphasized brisk pacing of the class, but Rowe (1974) recommended waiting 3 to 5 seconds when asking questions. Such contradictions raised the danger that teachers and staff developers would simply select whichever opinion they wanted to follow or, worse yet, see all research as invalid. Another barrier to appropriately using this research was that it was difficult for teachers and staff developers to find original research reports rather than reports which presented all the contextual details of findings only.

The current era in research on teaching began in the mid-1970s. Researchers began to give more attention to how the process and product variables were also influenced by contextual variables such as students' differences; class, school, and community characteristics; and teachers' developmental level or cognitive complexity. It has become clear that good teaching is not simply a matter of performing a prescribed set of behaviors. Teachers are now seen as instructional decision makers who, moment-by-moment, juggle a huge amount of information regarding context, students, subject matter, instructional processes, and outcomes. This view allows us to ask more complex questions today about effective teaching such as, "What factors should one consider when making instructional decisions about these particular learners, this content, and these instructional goals?" The goal for today's staff development programs is to help practitioners *know when and why to do what.*

Using Research as a Conceptual Tool
to Enhance Teachers' Decision Making

We will present two research topics use in this section from the recent research on teaching as illustrations of inquiry-oriented staff
development for classroom teachers: classroom management and cooperative learning.

Classroom Management

Early observational research in classrooms (Fisher et al., 1980) indicated that time-on-task is an important predictor of student achievement. Later studies pursued a deeper understanding of how some teachers manage to get such high time-on-task in their classrooms. This line of research has yielded much that is useful to teachers, supervisors, and leaders. It has not been disseminated in a "canned," prescriptive workshop series and is a fertile topic for inquiry-oriented staff development. Almost all teachers are willing to experiment with a few techniques to improve their students' involvement in learning.

Figure 9.1 presents a synopsis of research elements related to classroom management. It identifies variables, questions, and data-collection methods that teachers can use when inquiring into their own classroom management.

Figure 9.1
Classroom Management Research Elements

Possible Constructs/Variables
* Engaged time
* Monitoring
* Success rate
* Praise
* Teaching of rules and procedures
* Transition time
* Accountability
* Time spent on academics
* Active teaching

Possible Research Questions
* If I monitor students more during transitions, does time on task increase?
* If I praise Johnny in specific ways, does his work improve?
* If I teach and practice class rules, does behavior improve?
* How much time do my students spend actively involved with me, with peers, or on independent work in contrast to time spent off-task?

Data Collection Methods
* On task/off-task observation with coding system
* Interview regarding rules
* Audiotaping of a lesson with coding of success rate
* Time allocated to various activities
* Student performance on quizzes
* Running narrative of praise statements

In the late 1970s, a team of researchers at the University of Texas at Austin (Emmer et al., 1980) began to study how teachers achieve high time-on-task. They had a hunch that much of what accounted for a smooth-running classroom occurred at the beginning of the year, so they sent researchers into 27 3rd grade classrooms to use a guided observation system to record almost everything that occurred during the first three weeks. They also sent observers into the same classroom periodically during the school year to observe management and time-on-task. The researchers then contrasted seven more-effective with seven less-effective managers who were selected on the basis of student achievement gain and attitude and a composite of management indicators. The researchers found that although both groups introduced rules at the beginning of the year, the effective managers created a workable system of rules and taught them systematically to students.

The next step was to conduct an experiment where a group of teachers attended two workshops to help them improve their classroom management. At a workshop held before the school year, teachers received a manual that presented the research methods and detailed descriptions of the more effective and less effective managers' teaching. They attended a second workshop held three weeks into the school year. A similar group of teachers received no workshops or manuals. The group that participated in the workshops had significantly higher time-on-task throughout the school year.

The Texas researchers repeated the research sequence in junior high school classrooms and found a similar pattern for the beginning-of-the-year routines of more effective secondary teachers (Evertson & Emmer, 1982). They also conducted a staff development experiment that showed positive results for the group that received the workshops.

What is interesting about the Texas classroom management project is that the researchers presented the research methods and findings to the teachers without giving them prescriptions. Before the school year began, teachers were given narrative descriptions of the first days and weeks in several well-managed classrooms. The common characteristics of effective managers were identified, but the teachers were to choose — and experiment with — the strategies they selected. After the school year began, teachers were brought together to discuss what they were trying and how it worked. The researchers modeled a certain kind of thinking to the teachers — the thinking of a reflective educator who was still trying to make sense of classrooms and who did not claim to know exactly what works.

In contrast, note what happens when a workshop leader picks up only the research summary and takes the findings to teachers. Little background (sample, context) is given about the research. Teachers are given the findings in prescription form, models are provided, practice is given, and coaches go to classrooms to see if teachers are "doing it right."

There is much more to good teaching than just using a particular strategy **accurately.** *The teacher must use the strategy* **appropriately.**

In an ideal situation, teachers are "walked through" the research design; findings are discussed in light of the design, the context, and the sample; and findings are critiqued in terms of their applicability to the teachers' circumstances. After teachers are helped to perform the desired skills, they are encouraged to formulate questions about the effects of the new technique on students. Then teachers experiment with the new skills, observing and recording the impact on their students. They return to the workshop (quickly becoming an "inquiry-shop") to discuss what they have discovered about themselves, their teaching, and their students. They refine their new strategies, clarify new questions, and go out to tinker further with their teaching.

The latter approach, although more time-consuming, will produce an inquiry and reflection-oriented teacher who can then transfer those skills of analysis and experimentation to other classroom and school situations. There are many technical skills of teaching that need to be learned: explaining, modeling, and questioning, for example. But these skills have no lasting impact unless the teacher knows when and how to apply them.

Cooperative Learning

Two groups of researchers have examined cooperative learning during the 1970s and 1980s (Slavin, 1980; Johnson & Johnson, 1979). Cooperative learning differs from individualized and competitive learning, two predominant patterns in schools today. In cooperative learning, students are assigned to heterogeneous groups to complete a task that promotes interdependence. Children are helped to learn by the others and held individually accountable for their learning. The research has been conducted with both special and regular-education elementary and secondary students. Figure 9.2 presents the variables, questions, and data collection methods that could be used to explore this topic.

The cooperative learning researchers wanted to understand what happens when students teach each other. They recognized the problems of the traditional forms of group work: one student would do most of the work and the learning. Researchers observed small groups and experimented with different group activities and task structures to develop several different cooperative learning strategies. They then asked teachers to use these strategies while the researchers observed and measured attitudes, achievement scores, and higher-level thinking.

Some of the positive results of using cooperative learning include acceptance of others who are different, higher-level reasoning, intrinsic motivation, critical thinking, language development, self-acceptance, and collaborative skills.

An inquiry-oriented staff development program on cooperative learning would involve considerable time examining how the researchers conducted the research and how cooperative learning was defined and measured. Teachers then would receive several examples and observe good modeling of how the technique works. They might role-play the use of a particular strategy or design a lesson plan for use during the next week. After teachers had something concrete to try out, they would be helped to find ways to gather data to study their use of cooperative learning.

A good inquiry activity for teachers just beginning to use cooperative learning is recording the discussion of one group in their classroom. Teachers could listen carefully to answer such process questions: Are students participating equally? Are the task directions clear and appropriate? Where are students having problems? How can I set up the task better the next time? How are students reacting to each other?

Figure 9.2
Cooperative Learning Research Elements

Major Constructs/Variables

* Task structure
* Cooperative learning student behaviors
* Social skills
* Student higher level thinking
* Student willingness to cooperate with others

Possible Research Questions

* What cooperative behaviors are used by my students when they work in groups?
* Do I see any changes in students' levels of thinking as they work more in cooperative interdependent?

Data Collection Methods

* Observation of groups with coding of interaction
* Audiotapes coded for social skills use
* Observation and coding of student involvment
* Tests of higher-level thinking

Later, after a teacher has worked out many of the "bugs" of a strategy and students are accustomed to it, the teacher can ask questions about impact: Does this help students' thinking more? Are my lower achievers benefiting from this? Are biases about "smart" and "dumb" students fading? What other types of lessons does this work for? Does this seem to work better than direct teaching for certain topics?

Most teachers ask such questions naturally but often lack the tools and experience to systematically address them. In single-event staff development, there is little opportunity to follow up on such questions. More opportunities exist in multiple-session training, but the leaders often want to rush on to the next topic rather than spend time helping teachers analyze how they are using the ideas from the last workshop.

Staying with one topic long enough to allow teachers to inquire into the effects of a strategy is necessary for inquiry-oriented staff development. A portion of each workshop can be spent clarifying research questions and variables and discussing data collection strategies. A teacher might conduct a small study that could be reported to the other teachers. For example, a teacher could study the participation and communication skills of two low-achieving students as the use of cooperative learning increased during the semester.

Teachers are now seen as instructional decision makers who, moment-by-moment, juggle a huge amount of information regarding context, students, subject matter, instructional processes, and outcomes.

Other Research-Based Topics on Teaching

The teaching of higher-level thinking has been a predominate research topic for the past several years. There are many good sources that teachers or staff developers may wish to consult: Costa (1985), Raths et al. (1986) Wadsworth (1978) and Carr (1987).

Teacher expectations involve differential treatment of students based on expectations for student success. This phenomenon has been fascinating to teachers who are puzzled by the lack of equality of opportunity in the classroom. Some excellent sources are Good and Brophy (1987), Good (1981), and Kerman (1979).

Student self-esteem and moral development also concern many teachers. Helpful references are Beane & Lipke (1986), and Reimer et al. (1983).

A technical and thorough reference for recent research on teaching is *The Handbook on Research of Teaching* (Wittrock, 1986). It contains sections on the theory and method of research, research on teaching and teachers, the social and institutional context of teaching, adapting teaching to differences among learners, and research on the teaching of different subjects and grade levels.

Using Research on Instructional
Supervision, Coaching, and Mentoring

Today many districts are involved in staff development programs that feature classroom supervision, peer observation, team planning, mentor relationships, and research-based teacher assessment. Participants in such programs may be principals, teacher-mentors, department heads, or curriculum directors. Research related to these areas has emphasized observation systems, conference techniques, clinical supervision, and other supervisory models. Recently, two new themes have emerged: the criteria and processes used to assess teacher growth and matching types of supervision with teachers' individual characteristics such as experience or conceptual level.

The task of teacher assessment raises the question of how research should be used in supervision. Those involved in supervision, coaching, and mentoring should have a strong grasp of research on teaching and learning. But if research is presented prescriptively in "research-says-all-teachers-should . . . ." statements, then teacher reflection, analysis, and experimentation are stunted. To avoid this situation, supervisors and mentors may wish to use various strategies to encourage teachers to inquire into teaching. Asking questions such as "What would happen if . . . ?" or "What are some other ways of doing . . . ?" may help encourage such experimentation.

The goal for today's staff development programs is to help practitioners "know when and why to do what."

Clearly, however, supervisors, mentors, and coaches need to understand more than research on teaching and learning. They also need to understand the processes of supervision. Consider a specific example: Carl Glickman's (1981) developmental supervision.

Developmental supervision arose from Glickman's work with teachers and supervisors at the University of Georgia. His approach is built on two assumptions: (a) knowledge of stages of development in children, adolescents, adults, and teachers can be useful in supervision, and (b) the important question in research on supervision is not which model is best overall, but which approach is best for a particular individual.

A major contribution of Glickman's work is a synthesis of revelant research that has become a model for analyzing supervision. The model shows relationships among teacher characteristics (i.e., levels of commitment and abstract thinking), supervisory orientations, and supervisory behaviors. Figure 9.3 presents some of the elements related to this research.

A principals' support group provides an example of how Glickman's ideas can be used by a principal (Sarah) to supervise two first-year English teachers (Jerry and Anne) in a high school. During one of the principals' "Friday Afternoon Club" support meetings, the group discussed Glickman's ideas. The principals examined how researchers defined and

Figure 9.3
Developmental Supervision Research Elements

Major Constructs/Variables
* Teacher level of commitment
* Teacher level of abstract thinking
* Teacher vs. supervisor responsibility
* Supervisory behaviors
* Supervisory beliefs
* Supervisory orientation

Possible Research Questions
* What is this teacher's apparent level of commitment and of abstract thinking?
* What type of supervisory orientation and behaviors would be congruent with these teacher characteristics?
* What are the supervisor's beliefs?
* What supervisory behaviors are actually used by the supervisor and this teacher in their interaction?
* What are the corresponding levels of satisfaction and apparent productivity of such supervisory interaction from each person's perspective?

Data Collection Methods
* Semi-structured interviews
* Supervisory beliefs inventory
* Audiotapes of supervisory interaction

measured levels of commitment and abstract thinking. They were cautioned to use a flexible, trial-and-error approach to identifying their beginning teachers' characteristics. They were also encouraged to invite the new teachers to identify their own supervisory style preferences.

As Sarah chatted with Jerry and Anne during August and September, she developed tentative hunches about their professional backgrounds, interests, and needs. Sarah drew them into conversations about the basics of effective teaching and found that they both wanted to focus on classroom management. She consulted Glickman's work to clarify what she was learning about each person and to develop individualized strategies for working with each of them. She also shared her experiences in her principals' support group and got their ideas about supervisory approaches for the two teachers.

Jerry had difficulty making his abstract vision of "the classroom as a place of mutual respect and enthusiasm for learning" a reality. He was vague about his expectations for students and did not know how to teach routines and rules. Because of Jerry's lack of confidence and clarity, Sarah used a directive style of supervision with him. She assisted him in exploring the Evertson and Emmer (1982) classroom management research methods, questions, data sources, and findings. With much guidance and feedback from Sarah, Jerry experimented with ways to teach students the expected behavior. As months passed, he had created a satisfactory learning environment.

In contrast to Jerry, Anne was very clear in her expectations and projected an air of calmness and sincerity with her students. She was concerned, however, with their competitiveness and with some students' low self-esteem in such an environment. Sarah chose a collaborative supervisory style with Anne because of her sophisticated analysis of the situation. Sarah directed Anne to the research on cooperative learning and self-esteem and encouraged her to share the results of what she was trying out in her class. As months passed, Anne created a cooperative environment where students' self-esteem and confidence were enhanced.

Sarah periodically audiotaped her sessions with Jerry and Anne to check on her adaptations of Glickman's ideas. The tapes also helped clarify the goals and procedures they used. Sarah asked the two teachers to reflect on their experience with her supervision and with their first year of teaching. She often consulted her principals' support group to check her ideas and to get new ideas. She even asked one colleague to listen to a tape of a conference to get an impartial reaction about her application of Glickman's ideas.

As Sarah worked with Jerry and Anne, she revised her original hunches about their interests and needs. She found that Glickman's model helped her refine her approach with each teacher and understand better how and why they reacted as they did. She vowed to continue learning about valuable approaches to leadership and supervision with the principals' support group. She also began to learn about other approaches to supervising different types of teachers by watching a colleague as he observed and conducted conferences with two teachers.

Supervision is only one area of staff development for administrators and teacher leaders. Other areas include evaluation, school improvement, communication, conflict resolution, conducting meetings, leadership style, and curriculum. (The annotated bibliography at the end of this chapter includes research-based sources on many of these topics that may be of interest to supervisors and leaders.)

Teachers experiment with the new skills, observing and recording the impact on their students. They return to the workshop (quickly becoming an "inquiry-shop") to discuss what they have discovered about themselves, their teaching, and their students.

Recommendations and Conclusions

Research is a valuable foundation for the content of staff development programs, but it should be provided to participants as a tool for inquiry into practice rather than as a source of rules. The following are recommendations to staff developers who wish to use research-based content in their staff development programs. In addition, guiding questions for assessing your program are displayed in Figure 4 and competencies are listed in Figure 5.

1. **Avoid the phrases "research says" and "research shows."** Provide information about how the research was conducted and the kinds of students, teachers, and schools

involved in the study. With this information, participants can decide how they can adapt the research to their own situation.

2. **Encourage hypothesizing about why the research results turned out the way they did.** Such a task helps participants answer the questions: Why and how would this work if I tried it?

3. **Encourage experimentation with the research-based techniques to see how effective they are in the work setting.** Ask participants to pick one or two new things to try out before the next workshop or meeting. Ask them to be ready to report to the group what happened, why, and what they learned.

4. **Invite participants to discuss when the research-based technique probably would not work well.** For example, teachers could discuss when it would and would not be a good idea to give hints after a wrong answer ("delving," see Kerman, 1979).

5. **Encourage participants to discuss how they are already doing the things research indicates are effective.** Let the more expert participants share the "nuts and bolts" of their effective practices with others. For example, after presenting Evertson & Emmer's (1982) research questions, methods, and findings, principals could share how they help teachers establish their beginning-of-the-year routines.

6. **Use action research techniques to help participants do more in-depth investigations in their schools or classes.** Help participants form questions about their teaching, supervision, or leadership. Provide observation forms and simple methods of analysis for participants to use in informal inquiry.

Staying with one topic long enough to allow teachers to inquire into the effects of a strategy is necessary for inquiry-oriented staff development.

School workplace conditions have a big influence on the potential for and success of inquiry-oriented staff development. An increasing number of schools and districts are using effective teaching research findings to evaluate teachers. Teachers are expected to use a small set of effective practices when they are observed by administrators. Such a view inhibits the spirit of inquiry, risk taking, and experimentation. It also contradicts what we believe about teaching as reflective instructional decision making.

Schools need to nurture inquiry-oriented staff development. It is hoped that this goal will be reached as administrators are trained to be instructional leaders, as better-prepared teachers enter the work force, as staff development comes to be seen as a vehicle toward enlightened decision making, and as practitioners come to see that research is much more complex than just a series of findings.

Our schools and society are getting more complicated each year. In the 21st century, teachers will need to juggle a huge amount of information as they make decisions based on their own professional knowledge, compiled through extensive, research-guided experimentation and risk taking. Simple "research-says" prescriptions will not be enough.

Figure 9.4
Assessing Your Program

1. Do I make an effort to get my professional training from those who have done or who thoroughly know research on the topic I'm studying? Do I know the full history of the research on this topic along with its strengths and weaknesses?

2. Do I provide information for teachers about how the research was done, such as content area and sample description, so that we can discuss its appropriate application?

3. Do I read current research in my area of expertise?

4. Do I engage in inquiry on my own practice as I conduct staff development activities? For example, do I reflect on redesigning a workshop or consider using action research in my program evaluations?

5. Do I need to be better acquainted with qualitative and quantitative research methods so I can help participants engage in inquiry activities?

6. Do I encourage participants to take a few ideas from the workshop, experiment with them, and collect data on their effects?

7. Do I encourage and arrange support groups where teachers and leaders can engage in group learning and problem solving? Do I know how to create and lead such a group?

8. Do I plan comprehensive staff development activities that include more than training? That is, do I try to provide opportunities for practitioners to develop skills and ideas through peer coaching, support groups, individual study, and other intellectually challenging ways?

Figure 9.5
Competencies

1. Encourages experimentation and analysis.
2. Is warm, supportive, and nurturing for risk-taking.
3. Sees practitioners as capable of reflection and analysis.
4. Enjoys inquiry into teaching and learning in classrooms, schools, and training settings.
5. Facilitates rather than dominates when participant sharing and reflection are appropriate.
6. Is open-minded and willing to see many approaches to teaching as appropriate for varying conditions.
7. Is research-literate: understands various methods of research along with their strengths and weaknesses.
8. Understands in-depth the research on adult learning, student learning, teaching, supervision, leadership, staff development, and change processes.
9. Can model and guide inquiry processes for practitioners -- from simple "tinkering with teaching" to full-blown action research.
10. Understands the history of philosophies of curriculum, research, and teacher education.

References

Beane, J. & Lipke, R. (1986). *Self-concept, self-esteem, and the curriculm.* New York: Teachers College Press.

Carr, E. (1987). *Teaching reading as thinking.* Alexandria, VA: Association for Supervision and Curriculum Development.

Clark, C., & Peterson, P. (1986). Teachers' thought processes. In M. Wittrock (Ed.), *Handbook of research on teaching* (3rd ed.). New York: MacMillan.

Costa, A. (Ed.). (1985). *Developing minds: A resource book for teaching thinking.* Alexandria, VA: Association for Supervision and Curriculum Development.

Emmer, E., Evertson, C., & Anderson, L. (1980). Effective classroom management at the beginning of the school year. *Elementary School Journal, 80,* 219-231.

Evertson, C., & Emmer, E. (1982). Effective management at the beginning of the year in junior high school classes. *Journal of Educational Psychology, 74,* 485-498.

Fisher, C., Berliner, D., Filby, N., Marliave, R., Cahen, L., & Dishaw, M. (1980). Teaching behavior, academic learning time, and student achievement: An overview. In C. Denham & A. Lieberman (Eds.), *Time to Learn.* Washington, DC: National Institute of Education.

Glickman, C. (1981). *Developmental supervision: Alternative practices for helping teachers improve instruction.* Alexandria, VA: Association for Supervision and Curriculum Development.

Good, T. (1981). Teacher expectations and student perceptions: A decade of research. *Educational Leadership, 38*(5), 415-522.

Good, T., & Brophy, J. (1987). *Looking in classrooms.* New York: Harper & Row.

Hunter, M. (1985, Jan.). What's wrong with Madeline Hunter? *Educational Leadership, 42*(5), 57-70.

Johnson, D., & Johnson, R. (1979). Conflict in the classroom: controversy and learning. *Review of Educational Research, 49,* 51-70.

Joyce, B., & Showers, B. (1983). *Power in staff development through research on training.* Alexandria, VA: Association for Supervision and Curriculum Development.

Kerman, S. (1979, June). Teacher expectations and student achievement. *Phi Delta Kappan, 60*(10), 716-718.

Kounin, J. (1970). *Discipline and group management in classrooms.* New York: Holt, Rinehart, and Winston.

Raths, L., Wasserman, S., Jonas, A., & Rothstein, A. (1986). *Teaching for thinking.* New York: Teachers College Press.

Reimer, J., Paolitto, D., & Hersch, R. *Promoting moral development: From Piaget to Kohlberg (2nd ed.).* New York: Longman.

Rowe, M. (1974). Wait time and rewards as instructional variables. *Journal of Research in Science Teaching, 11,* 81-94.

Ryans, D. (1960). *Characteristics of teachers.* Washington, DC: American Council on Education.

Schon, D. (1983). *The reflective practitioner.* New York: Basic Books.

Schon, D. (1987). *Educating the reflective practitioner.* San Francisco: Jossey Bass.

Simmons, J.M., & Schuette, M.K. (1988). Strengthening teacher reflective decision making. *Journal of Staff Development, 9*(3).

Simmons, J., & Sparks, G. (1985). Using research to develop professional thinking about teaching. *Journal of Staff Development, 6*(1), 106-116.

Slavin, R. (1980). Cooperative learning. *Review of Educational Research, 50,* 315-342.

Wadsworth, B. (1978). *Piaget for the classroom teacher.* New York: Longman.

Wittrock, M.C. (Ed.). (1986). *Handbook of research on teaching* (3rd ed.). New York: Macmillan.

Provide information about how the research was conducted and the kinds of students, teachers, and schools involved in the study.

Chapter 10

Theory, Research and Practice Foundations of Staff Development

Theory, research, and recommendations from practice regarding the processes of school improvement have added to an emerging knowledge base for staff development. We are just beginning to understand how to orchestrate the necessary changes . . . to make school improvement a reality.

Albert A. Bertani
and
Linda S. Tafel

Although research literature is replete with descriptions of effective schools, educators still are learning how a school become effective. They are just beginning to understand how to orchestrate the necessary changes in curriculum, pedagogy, and organizational processes to make school improvement a reality (Lieberman & Rosenholtz, 1987).

Since Sarason (1971) first conceptualized the enormous social and cultural complexities of changing schools, knowledge of school improvement has continued to expand. Theory, research, and recommendations from practice have added to this knowledge base. One lesson about school improvement provides the foundation for this chapter: "Substantial, continuous staff development is essential to the improvement of schooling and, equally important, to the development of the capability for the continuous renewal of education" (Joyce, 1981, p. 117). Using context, content, and process as organizers, this chapter highlights, discusses, and challenges the existing and emerging knowledge bases for staff development.

What We Know About the Context
for Staff Development

Educational systems are highly complex organizations composed of district-level hierarchies, individual schools with their own cultures, and unique individuals — students, teachers, and administrators. Failure to acknowledge these organizational complexities results in lopsided efforts to effect growth, improvement, and renewal. If staff development is viewed exclusively as a tool for developing the individuals in a school or district, it is "half a loaf" at best (Goodlad, 1983). Staff development must be balanced by organizational development to enhance the "ecology" of an entire system.

Throughout most of the 20th century, educators have explained how schools work with a rational-bureaucratic model that promotes a vertical, top-down, linear approach. This view now is being reexamined, based on a growing understanding of educational organizations (Patterson, et al., 1986).

An Emerging Professional Model

The emerging alternative to the rational-bureaucratic model is a nonrational-professional model. This model questions the organizational relationships between goals, structures, activities, and outcomes (Patterson, et al., 1986). It identifies the weakness of the rational-bureaucratic model by recognizing that "the world of work consists mostly of horizontal relationships" (Cleveland, 1985, p.9). Miles (1979) identifies the following salient features of schools using the nonrational-professional model.

* School goals are vague and lend themselves to multiple interpretations.
* Many teaching styles develop in the process of integrating school goals (Lortie, 1975).
* Classroom teachers are both constrained by and autonomous of school leaders.
* Schools are actually organizations of loosely-tied classrooms (Weick, 1982).
* Each school has a unique culture (Sarason, 1971).
* Schools and individual teachers go through stages as they cope with new ideas (Hall & Loucks, 1978).

The shift from rational-bureaucratic to nonrational-professional challenges us to rethink the traditional view of how educational organizations function. In the nonrational-professional model, leadership by knowledge replaces leadership by authority, participative decision making replaces bureaucratic directives, high expectations replace accountability, and inquiring behavior replaces mandated behavior (Goodlad, 1987).

The nonrational-professional model is an ecological model that differs sharply from the factory-production orientation of the rational-bureaucratic model. As the term ecological implies, this new model is concerned with relationships of living things — individuals — to each other and to their environments — schools and districts. An ecological perspective emphasizes the need to provide staff and organization development for individuals and schools and to promote and maintain a healthy ecosystem districtwide.

Context for District and School-Focused
Staff Development

Chapters 1 and 2 in this book described district-level and school-focused staff development. Although each discusses staff development from different organizational perspectives, their content is intimately connected because staff development at any level affects relationships within a system.

Organization development promotes the effectiveness of the organization while supporting staff development designed for individuals (Dillon-Peterson, 1981). Generally, organization development addresses the adequacy and appropriateness of leadership, decision making, problem solving, conflict management, communication, and planning (Schmuck, et al., 1977). These issues determine the ecological balance of relationships in an educational organization.

Educators have explained how schools work with a rational-bureaucratic model that promotes a vertical, top-down, linear approach. This view now is being reexamined.

Assumptions

As noted in Chapter 2, certain assumptions about staff and organization development undergird school-focused efforts. Assumptions that demonstrate the relationship between staff and organization development include:

* Significant change takes considerable time (Crandall, 1983).
* Positive school climate is essential for successful staff development (Chamberlin, 1971; Zagarmi, 1981).
* Effective development requires personal and group commitment to new practices (Berman & Pauley, 1985; Sparks, 1983).
* Educators need to be actively involved as learners (Arends, et al., 1980; Lawerence, 1974; Roy, 1987).

Goal Alignment

Organizational issues related to centralizing or decentralizing staff development responsibilities deserve special consideration. The goal-setting processes for individuals, schools, and school districts are crucial in determining the locus of responsibility for staff development. Goals serve at least three purposes. They are a source of legitimacy, a source of direction, and a basis for evaluation (Dornbusch & Scott, 1975; Perrow, 1970). Consequently, organizations must pay special attention to the relationships among goals set by individuals, schools, and districts.

Effective organization development should be the glue for an organization during change. Development should deal with goal alignment, what is to be done, how it is to be done, communication, criteria for decision making, and the development of individual and organizational commitment (Argyris, 1970; Berman & McLaughlin, 1978; Nadler, 1977; Stewart, 1973; Weisborg, 1976). Individually, each issue has tremendous potential for positively or negatively affecting staff and organization development. Collectively, these issues comprise critical decision-points as goals, activities, and programs are linked.

Whether a district uses a centralized or decentralized approach, staff development and organization development should be equal partners. District-level and school-focused goals must be coordinated with individual goals to support growth, improvement, and renewal that are equally beneficial for each level of organization. This coordination is the only way to ensure a balance in the ecology of the educational system.

The Context for Individually-Focused Staff Development

School organizations consist of individuals interacting within formal and informal groups (Roark & Davis, 1981). These individuals differ in complex ways as adult learners.

Organizations must pay special attention to the relationships among goals set by individuals, schools, and districts.

Developmental variables exist in the areas of cognition and interpersonal orientation (Bents & Howey, 1981). Staff development activities and programs can be enhanced if they take into account how adults learn and develop (see Chapter 3).

Theoretical Principles

According to Knowles (1978), the following principles constitute the foundation of theory on adult learning:

1. Adults are motivated to learn as they experience needs and interests that learning will satisfy; therefore, these needs and interests are appropriate starting points for organizing adult learning activities.
2. Adult orientation to learning is life-centered; therefore, the appropriate units for organizing adult learning are life situations, not subjects.
3. Experience is the richest resource for adult learning; therefore, the core methodology of adult education is the analysis of experience.
4. Adults have a deep need to be self-directing; therefore, the role of the teacher is to engage in a process of mutual inquiry rather than to transmit knowledge to adults and then evaluate their conformity to it.
5. Individual differences among people increase with age; therefore, adult education must make optimal provision for differences in style, time, place, and pace of learning (p. 31).

The traditional, rational-bureaucratic model views staff development as remediation (Krupp, 1986; Wood et al., 1981). This deficit, or defect, orientation is not consistent with the emerging nonrational-professional model. School renewal and improvement require a developmental perspective consistent with the research on adult learning and development. Considerable research exists to support this orientation to growth.

Adult developmental theorists can be divided into two basic groups: age theorists and stage theorists (Chickering, 1974). Age theorists are interested in the concerns and problems common to most adults at various ages of their lives. Stage theorists are interested in the qualitative differences in an individual's thinking at various points in development, not necessarily related to age. Berrin, Levinson, Gould, Sheehy, and Krupp (see Chapter 3) have contributed to the knowledge base for age theorists. Piaget, Kohlberg, Hunt, Sprinthall, Loevinger, and Perry have contributed to the knowledge base for stage theorists. Staff developers must remember that adult development is a continuing growth process. An individual's developmental level is not a static classification; it represents an individual, current, preferred mode of operation (Hunt & Sullivan, 1974).

Research on adult cognition highlights the developmental differences in adults (See Kitchener, 1977; Kuhn, et al., 1971; Neimark, 1975; Tomlinson-Keasy, 1972). An individual's interpersonal development also plays an important role for participants in staff development (See Harvey et al., 1961; Loevinger, 1976; Oja, 1977).

Whether a district uses a centralized or decentralized approach, staff development and organization development should be equal partners.

Krupp discusses issues and practical implications of adult learning and development in Chapter 3. Her reflections reemphasize the need for staff developers to use research on adult learning and development. Staff development will be maximized if planning and implementation accommodate developmental differences.

Linking Individual Staff Development and Organization Development

Research and theory are the foundations for linking staff development and organization development. Individual development and organization development are dependent correlates. Within the context of school improvement, staff and organization development are "complementary human processes, inextricably interwoven, dynamic, interactive, nonlinear, and incredibly complex" (Dillon-Peterson, 1981, p. 3).

The unique contributions of each are described by Roark and Davis (1981): "Staff development attempts to achieve its goals primarily through an increase in individual competence while organization development concentrates on organizational competence" (p. 56). Integrating staff and organization development will produce activities and programs that:

* Develop district-level human resources through the development, coordination, administration, and monitoring of activities and programs (see Chapter 1).
* Improve educational practice by focusing on the individual school as the appropriate unit for change (see Chapter 2).
* Support individuals who have the inherent responsibility to define and achieve their own excellence (see Chapter 3).

Finally, Vaughn (1981) identifies a useful metaphor for the intricate and delicate relationships among districts, schools, and individuals. He describes the school as the fulcrum for change, supporting the influence beam containing the individual and district.

> At times the district will tip the beam in its direction by prescribing curricula, policies and procedures. At other times, teachers within schools close their doors and ignore district or even school influences, tipping the influence beam in their direction. To some extent, what happens at the school level can "balance" the two extremes (p. 14).

Growth, improvement, and renewal are achieved in educational organizations when staff developers integrate the vertical and horizontal relationships between and among individuals, schools, and district-level staff. A partnership to develop both the staff and the organization ensures the necessary ecological balance required in any relationship.

Historically, the content of staff development programs has been ill-defined. Assumptions have been made about what teachers know and what they need to know to do a better job in the classroom. These approaches have largely ignored knowledge that provides the basis for staff development programs.

What Should Be The Content of Staff Development Programs?

Historically, the content of staff development programs has been ill-defined. Program designers often have opted for generic, large-group presentations, hoping that staff members could latch on to a key idea or two that they could take back to their classrooms.

In more specific programs, the content for staff development programs has been determined by using the deficit, or defect, theory (Krupp, 1986; Wood et al., 1981). Assumptions have been made about what teachers know and what they need to know to do a better job in the classroom. These approaches have largely ignored knowledge that provides the basis for staff development programs. Several authors (Loucks-Horsley, 1987; Vaughan, 1981) have urged staff developers to base staff development practices on research, but there has been little elaboration about the appropriate content for staff development programs (see Chapter 9).

Categories of Content

Shulman's (1987) analysis of the major sources of teaching knowledge provides planners with guidelines for choosing content for staff development programs. Shulman identifies four general information sources:

* Scholarship in content disciplines
* The materials and setting of the institutionalized educational process
* Research on schooling, social organizations, human learning, teaching and development, and the other social and cultural phenomena that affect what teachers do
* The wisdom of practice itself (p. 8)

Scholarship in Content Disciplines

In discussing scholarship in content disciplines, Shulman (1987) notes that the "teacher has a special responsibility in relation to content knowledge, serving as the primary source of student understanding of subject matter" (p. 9). Without a solid foundation and current information in a subject, teachers may fail to communicate key ideas to their students. Teachers need a chance to identify their needs related to content knowledge and then take part in staff development programs to expand their knowledge. This is especially crucial for curricular areas in which an information explosion makes even the newest textbooks and workbooks obsolete.

Often veteran teachers are privy only to limited information about the total school organization and therefore do not understand their role or function within the system.

For teachers to increase their scholarship in content areas, several important assumptions about continuing professional growth need to pervade the staff development process. The process needs to acknowledge that teacher preparation is only part of a process of continuous learning. Knowledge in content areas is infinite rather than finite, and teachers and students will continue to explore new ideas and emerging information. Teachers will continue to reconcile new learnings with old and adjust their teaching of key concepts.

In the staff development process, teachers who risk identifying their own areas for improvement should be encouraged and supported in their efforts to expand their knowledge. Resource materials and people in the specific content areas should be available to teachers throughout their careers.

Educational Materials and Structures

Educational materials and structures call upon teachers to know the territory of teaching — to understand curricula, tests, school organization, and school budgets. The key issue here is how schooling works in a particular district. Knowledge about such topics allows the teacher to feel more in control of the work environment and able to align classroom goals and practices with those of the larger school organization. Often veteran teachers are privy only to limited information about the total school organization and therefore do not understand their role or function within the system. Staff development designed to inform staff members about district- and school-based procedures and practices and to involve staff members in decision making is essential (Sparks, 1983).

Scholarship in Educational Processes

Formal educational scholarship is mushrooming as educators attempt to better understand the processes of schooling, teaching, and learning. Shulman (1987) says that "the philosophical, critical, and empirical literature which can inform the goals, visions, and dreams of teachers is a major portion of the scholarly knowledge base of teaching" (p. 10). This broad definition of educational scholarship means that, in addition to being familiar with widely cited but often prescriptive teacher effectiveness research, teachers ought to reconsider research on learning and development and what happens when individual learners come together in the classroom.

Buchmann (1987) makes a strong case for using research findings both to inform teachers and to spark discussion. Such practice "aims to engage the mind and aids the growth and change of understanding" (p. 181). Buchmann argues that teachers must become more than passive consumers of research and move into active knowledge construction. Through inquiry into research on classroom

Teachers teaching teachers, teacher helpers, and peer coaching arrangements all stem from the belief that if one wants to know how to teach well, one must seek out the wise counsel of an able colleague.

teaching and through engaging in their own classroom research projects, teachers can add to the growing knowledge base (see Chapter 9).

Wisdom of Practice

Wisdom of practice, is "least codified of all" and centers around "the maxims that guide . . . the practice of able teachers" (Shulman, 1987, p. 11). Staff development programs need to do more than tap the strengths of veteran staff members or showcase highly visible teacher-leaders. These programs must move toward codifiying sound practices based on the knowledge held by able teachers.

The wisdom-of-practice notion that Shulman discusses has been at the heart of teacher education and staff development for many years. Teachers teaching teachers, teacher helpers, and peer coaching arrangements all stem from the belief that if one wants to know how to teach well, one must seek out the wise counsel of an able colleague. As staff development efforts are organized, however, these persons often are passed by. Informal networks among teachers may exist, but they may never be tapped and teacher leadership may remain largely undeveloped.

In addition to identifying their own staff development needs (Dillon-Peterson, 1986), teachers are capable of identifying their own strengths and the strengths of other able teachers. Teachers are capable of codifying their practice and helping others learn from their experiences and expertise. Drawing on these models of "pedagogical excellence" (Shulman, 1987, p. 20) to inform the practice of other teachers is an essential component of staff development.

Relationship Between Content and Context

Although Shulman's framework helps identify content for staff development, two important relationships between content and organization need to be acknowledged.

First is the reciprocal relationship between the context for staff development and its content. If the school organization envisions the teacher as an assembly-line implementer of prepackaged, teacher-proof curricular materials, then the notions of teacher as researcher, knowledge-creator, and holder of wisdom will probably be inappropriate. By examining Shulman's framework, basic assumptions about teachers, the role of teachers within the school, and the appropriate activities for staff development should be discussed during program planning. When a mismatch between content and context is found, an analysis and change of the context must take place before the content for staff development can be determined.

Second, the content of staff development programs must be directly and appropriately linked to those processes used to implement the program (see Chapter 5). Loucks-Horsley et al. (1987) have detailed 12 alternative approaches to teacher development, giving planners a variety of options to achieve their staff development goals. Each of the approaches, however, must be carefully analyzed in relation to the program content. By closely examining the knowledge base for staff development and identified teacher needs, a program "characterized by diversity of ideas, people, and support practices" (p. 21) is likely to result.

Process

Lingering images of the inservice model often influence and limit how staff development takes shape (Edelfelt, 1986). When the process involves discrete events or a series of activities for teachers, vestiges of the inservice-training model are present. The rational-bureaucratic orientation fostered the inservice-training model, placing teachers primarily in a passive-receptive role by stressing their weaknesses or deficits. In such a model, staff development is characterized by a "working-on" perspective (Lieberman, 1986).

The nonrational-professional orientation views staff development in two significantly different ways. First, the process of staff development focuses on the growth, improvement, and renewal of both the individual and the school organization. Second, the process of staff development is driven by content that is appropriate for and consistent with the identified needs of teachers. This model of staff development is characterized by a "working-with" perspective (Lieberman, 1986; Ward & Tikunoff, 1982).

A comparison of the assumptions regarding "working on" and "working with" is helpful for two reasons. These assumptions can help staff developers clarify their own beliefs about staff development, and can serve as benchmarks for assessing current staff development efforts (Bertani, et al. 1987). Table 10.1 contrasts characteristics of the outdated, "working on" model with the emerging "working with" model of staff development.

Table 10.1
Orientations to Staff Development

Assumptions of "working on" (Rational-Bureaucratic)	Assumptions of "working with" (Nonrational-Professional)
Ignores or assumes organizational context and dynamics	Acknowledges organizational frameworks and issues regarding organizational health
Ignores developmental perspectives on individual and organizational change	Acknowledges and uses theory on organization development, adult development, and personal and professional growth
Emphasizes vertical relationships	Emphasizes horizontal relationships
Defines target audience through deficits	Accepts teacher/learner "as is;" all teachers viewed as capable of improving, learning, changing
Programs tend to be generic	Staff development efforts are tailor-made; meeting district, school, and individual needs
Over-emphasis on quick-fix techniques and strategies	Thoughtful reflection, self-analysis and incremental change methodologies urged
Staff developer possesses special knowledge or "knows best what teachers need to know"	Experience of teachers acknowledged and used as integral part of the knowledge base
Product or competency-based orientation	Emphasis on people and process

After staff developers come to terms with their own beliefs about staff development, their actions should demonstrate a congruence between and among their beliefs, contextual issues, content considerations, and process decisions. A "working with" orientation to staff development is dynamic, evolving, and multi-dimensional, although this discussion presents a linear description of five specific planning stages that are essential decision-points in designing staff development programs.

How does the process of staff development begin to take shape? First, planners seek information about the context for staff development. Information about the district, schools, administrators, teachers, children, and community needs to be considered as the foundation for the entire process.

The second step is the careful examination of district and school goals. Successful staff development efforts have demonstrated that there must be a consistency between what teachers are asked to try and the goals of the school district or building. Planners will enhance their efforts to affect lasting change if staff development programs are closely linked to both the curriculum development process and the evaluation process of the organization (Lieberman & Rosenholtz, 1987).

A "working with" orientation to staff development is dynamic, evolving, and multi-dimensional.

Data gathered from a careful analysis of contextual factors plus school or district goals should guide staff developers as they determine the most appropriate content for their programs. Answering the question "What do teachers want to know or learn?" is the third step in planning. If content is planned with context issues and school or district goals clearly in mind, staff development will stem from individual and organizational needs. This "tailored" approach will ensure a match between and a commitment to school improvement through individual and organization development.

After decisions have been made about content, approaches for delivering the content may be determined. At this point, planners may look both inside and outside the school organization for resources to match the intent of the program. Once again, the approaches for delivering content must be consistent with organizational issues and goal statements.

We agree with the assessment of Loucks-Horsley et al.(1987): "There is no best combination of approaches, no best entry point for new staff development programs" (p. 43). Accordingly, staff developers need to be keenly aware of the wide variety of approaches available and the strengths and limitations of each, capitalize on human resources within the organization that can support staff development, and thoughtfully consider the use of external consultants and programs as resources.

It is not enough for staff developers to know about approaches for delivering staff development. Perhaps the most important aspect in the selection process is considering the evidence regarding the application of various approaches in school settings.

For each of the 12 approaches identified by Loucks-Horsley et al. (1987), researched-benefits have been assessed. Because we are only beginning to answer many questions about the effects of staff development approaches, we must use what we know while we continue to enlarge the theory base. From our analysis of "what's known," we do not believe that prescriptive approaches are appropriate. Staff developers need to examine a number of possible approaches that may be useful in tailoring staff development in a specific educational context.

The process of staff development should be characterized by a "working with" perspective. This approach would ensure the critical linkages between the context, content, and process in all staff development efforts. Sensitivity to the intricate relationships of these dimensions will enhance staff development efforts at all levels within the organization.

Final Reflections

Staff development has matured considerably over the past 20 years. Ever-expanding knowledge on the context, content, and process of staff development has helped us write a script that promotes growth, improvement, and renewal.

Understanding individual and organizational change provides the foundation for effective practice in staff development. Although theory, research, and practice have helped us become better informed about the barriers and bridges to school improvement (Lieberman & Rosenholtz, 1987), staff developers also must remember the special challenges of any developmental process.

Schlesinger (1986) reminds us of these challenges in *The Cycles of American History*.

> *Change is threatening. Innovation may seem an assault on the foundations of the universe . . . In art and science, the innovator has only to persuade one person: himself. But innovation in a democracy faces a still harder task: the innovator must persuade **others** to change **their** minds (p. 424).*

The challenges are clear. Staff developers must conceive, develop, nurture, and orchestrate district, school, and individual opportunities for growth, improvement, and renewal. Knowing about effective practice in staff development is not enough. Staff developers must use knowledge from theory, research, and practice as a foundation for planning, implementing, and evaluating staff development locally.

Once again, Schlesinger (1986) provides a useful description of the specialized responsibilities of the staff developer as leader.

> *Leadership is what makes the world go round. Love no doubt smooths the passage; but love is a transaction between consenting adults. Leadership — the capacity to inspire and mobilize masses of people — is a public transaction with history (p. 419).*

Knowledge without the passion to use it creatively to improve conditions becomes useless. If knowledge is to become power, it must become powerful through leadership.

References

Arends, R., Hersh, R., & Turner, J. (1980). *Conditions for promoting effective staff development*. Washington, DC: ERIC Clearinghouse on Teacher Education.

Argyris, C. (1970). *Intervention theory and method*. Reading, MA: Addison-Wesley.

Bents, R.H., & Howey, K.R. (1981). Staff development change in the individual. In B. Dillon-Peterson (Ed)., *Staff development/organizational development*. Alexandria, VA.: Association for Supervision and Curriculum Development.

Berman, P., & McLaughlin, M.W. (1978). *Federal programs supporting educational change: Implementing and sustaining innovations*. Washington DC: U.S. Office of Education, R-1589 No. 8 - HEW.

Berman, P., & Pauley, E.W. (1985). *Federal programs supporting educational changes: Factors affecting change*. Santa Monica, CA: Rand Corp.

Bertani, A., Tafel, L., Proctor, J., & Vydra, J. (1987, Spring). Teachers as leaders: A district plans for new roles, new directions. *Journal of Staff Development, 8*(2), 36-38.

Buchmann, M. (1987). Reporting and using educational research: Conviction or persuasion? In J.I. Goodlad, (Ed.), *The ecology of school renewal* (pp. 170-191). Chicago: University of Chicago Press.

Chamberlin, L.J. (1971). *Effective instruction through dynamic discipline*. Columbus, OH: Charles E. Merrill.

Chickering, A.K. (1974, December). *The educational needs of new learners: Implications for liberal arts colleges*. Paper presented at the East Central Colleges Consortium Conference on the New Learners.

Cleveland, H. (1985). *The knowledge executive*. New York: E.P. Dutton.

Crandall, D. (1983, Nov.). The teacher's role in school improvement. *Educational Leadership, 18*, 15-18.

Dillon-Peterson, B. (1981). Staff development/organization development-perspective 1981. In B. Dillon-Peterson, (Ed.). *Staff development/organization development*, pp. 1-10. Alexandria, VA: Association for Supervision and Curriculum Development.

Dillon-Peterson, B. (1986). Trusting teachers to know what's good for them. in K. Zumwalt, (Ed.). *Improving teaching*, pp. 29-35. Alexandria, VA: Association for Supervision and Curriculum Development.

Dornbush, S., & Scott, R.W. (1975). *Evaluation and the exercise of authority*. San Francisco: Jossey-Bass.

Edelfelt, R.A. (1986, Spring). Staff development in the next 10 years. *The Journal of Staff Development, 7*(1), 83-87.

Goodlad, J. I. (1983). The school as workplace. In G. Griffin, (Ed.). *Staff development*, (pp. 36-61). Chicago: University of Chicago Press.

Goodlad, J.I. (1987). Structures, process and an agenda. In J.I. Goodlad, (Ed.). *The ecology of school renewal*, (pp.1-19). Chicago: University of Chicago Press.

Hall, G., & Loucks, S. (1978, September). Teacher concerns as a basis for facilitating and personalizing staff development. *Teachers College Record, 80*, 36-53.

Harvey, O.J., Hunt, D.E., & Schroder, H.M. (1961). *Conceptual systems and personality organization*. New York: John Wiley.

Hunt, D.E., & Sullivan, E.V. (1974). *Between psychology and education*. Hinsdale, IL: Dryden.

Joyce, B. (1981). A memorandum for the future. In B. Dillon-Peterson, (Ed.). *Staff development/organization development* (pp. 113-127). Alexandria, VA: Association for Supervision and Curriculum Development.

Kitchener, K.S. (1977). *Intellectual development in late adolescents and young adults: Reflective judgment and verbal reasoning.* Unpublished doctoral dissertation, University of Minnesota, Minneapolis.

Knowles, M. (1978). *The adult learner: A neglected species.* Houston: Gulf.

Krupp, J.A. (1986). Staff development: Problems that reveal solutions. *Insights into professional development.* Hartford, CT: Connecticut Organization for Professional Development.

Kuhn, D., Langer, J., Kohlberg, L., & Haan, N. (1971). *The development of formal-operational thought: Its relation to moral judgment.* Unpublished manuscript.

Lawrence, G. (1974). *Patterns of effective inservice education.* Unpublished manuscript, Florida State Department of Education.

Lieberman, A. (1986). Collaborative work. *Educational Leadership, 43,* 4-8.

Lieberman, A., & S. Rosenholtz. (1987). The road to school improvement: Barriers and bridges. In J.I. Goodlad, *The ecology of school renewal* (pp. 79-98). Chicago: University of Chicago Press.

Loevinger, J. (1976). *Ego development.* San Francisco: Jossey-Bass.

Lortie, D.C. (1975). *Schoolteacher: A sociological study.* Chicago: University of Chicago Press.

Loucks-Horsley, S., Harding, C.K, Arbuckle, M.A., Murray, L.B., Dubea, C., & Williams, M.K. (1987). *Continuing to learn: A guidebook for teacher development.* Andover, MA: The Regional Laboratory for Educational Improvement of the Northeast and Islands.

Miles, M. (1979). *Common properties of school in context: The backdrop for knowledge utilization and school improvement.* Washington, DC: National Institute of Education.

Nadler, D.A. (1977). *Feedback and organization development: Using data-based methods.* Reading, MA: Addison-Wesley.

Neimark, E.D. (1975). Intellectual development during adolescence. In F.D. Horowitz (Ed.). *Review of Child Development Research.* Chicago: University of Chicago Press.

Oja, S. (1977). *A cognitive-structural approach to adult ego, moral and conceptual development through inservice teacher education.* Unpublished doctoral dissertation, University of Minnesota, Minneapolis.

Patterson, J.L., Purkey, S.C., & Parker, J.V. (1986). *Productive school systems for a non-rational world.* Alexandria, VA: Association for Supervision and Curriculum Development.

Perrow, C. (1970). *Organizational analysis: A sociological view.* Belmont, CA: Wadsworth.

Rourke, A.E., & Davis, W.E. (1981). Staff development and organizational development. In B. Dillon-Peterson (Ed.), *Staff development/organizational development.* Alexandria, VA: Association for Supervision and Curriculum Development.

Roy, P. (1987, February). Consumers guide to selecting staff development consultants. *The Developer, 2*(1), 8-9.

Sarason, S.B. (1971). *The culture of the school and the problem of change.* New York: Allyn and Bacon.

Schlesinger, A.M., Jr. (1986). *The cycles of American history.* Boston: Houghton Mifflin.

Schmuck, R., Runkel, P.J., Arends, J.H., & Arends, R.I. (1977). *The second handbook of organization development in schools.* Palo Alto, CA: Mayfield.

Shulman, L.S. (1987, February). Knowledge and teaching: Foundations of the new reform. *Harvard Educational Review, 57,* 1-23.

Sparks, G. M. (1983). Synthesis of research on staff development for effective teaching. *Educational Leadership, 41*(3), 65-72.

Stewart, B. (1973, June). What is organizational development and how does it apply to schools? *Education Canada, 13,* 19-21.

Tomlinson-Keasy, C. (1972). Formal operations in females from eleven to fifty-four years of age. *Developmental Psychology, 6,* 364.

Vaughan, J. (1981, Winter). Using research on teaching, schools and change to help staff development make a difference. *The Journal of Staff Development, 4*(2), 6-24.

Ward, B., & Tikunoff, J. (1982, February). *Collaborative research invited paper.* Paper presented at the Implications of Research on Teaching for Practice Conference, sponsored by the National Institute for Education, Washington, DC.

Weick, K.E. (1982, June). Administering education in loosely coupled systems. *Phi Delta Kappan, 63,* 673-676.

Weisborg, M.R. (1976). Organizational diagnosis: Six places to look for trouble with or without theory. *Group Organization Studies, 1,* 430-447.

Wood, F.H., Thompson, S.R., & Russell, F. (1981). Designing effective staff development programs. In B. Dillon-Peterson (Ed.). *Staff development/organization development* (pp. 59-92). Alexandria, VA: Association for Supervision and Curriculum Development.

Zagarmi, P. (1981, Summer). Leadership and school climate: A data-based approach to administrator training. *Journal of Staff Development, 2,* 93-115.

Staff development will stem from individual and organizational needs.

Chapter 11

Competencies of the Staff Developer

This chapter reports the competencies which distinguish between superior and average performing staff developers in Washington State. These competencies have implications for the training and development of staff developers.

Dian K. Castle

Although the previous chapters have added to the data base relevant to the role of staff developer, they have likewise heightened awareness of the void in the literature regarding the performance characteristics, competencies, of that role. Ellis includes a variety of tasks associated with the district-level staff developer as well as some of the knowledge and skills necessary to the performance of those tasks. Kent mentions the staff developer performing three roles: the change agent; the facilitator of learning; and the research. Loucks-Horsley emphasizes the change agent role while Marshall elaborates upon the program evaluator role. While most authors list the knowledge and skills necessary to perform basic tasks, non address those characteristics which distinguish superior performance from adequate performance (i.e., the competencies which underlie effective performance). Without clear performance criteria, school districts select, administrators supervise, educators train, and pruveyors consult to different (and sometimes even conflicting) images of the capabilities required to do the job.

This chapter reports the results and conclusions of research on staff development competencies. The study was funded by a grant from the Lynne Chidley Foundation of the National Staff Development Council (NDSC). Data were gathered by interview and survey of superior and average performing staff developers, as nominated by peers and recommended by supervisors. Competencies which distinguished superior from average performance will be examined in three areas: the roles/tasks of staff developers, the technical skills necessary to perform those roles; and the attributes associated with an individual's success within the organizational context.

These results are summarized and implications for the training and development of staff developers will be discussed. The Figures present the complete results of the competency study.

What is Competency?

Competency is the knowledge, skill, attitude, motive, behavior, self-image, social role, trait, and/or intellectual strategy that underlies effective performance. Performance characteristics are competencies when they exist in a role in an organizational setting and are performed to an established standard. Competencies are not defined as components of a given job; they are special characteristics of people who do the job best. Although they are identifiable and measurable, they are invisible except through behaviors which reflect the competency. Therefore, competencies are known only through their application.

Variations in job performance can be attributed to the degree to which individuals execute certain critical tasks on the job. A critical task is defined as a behavior that is (a) considered important by peers, supervisors, and subordinates, (b) has a wide variation among its performers, and (c) allows this variability to be easily perceived by others. Performance on a series of critical tasks is predictive of performance on the job. The degree to which an individual performs a critical task well is a function of the degree of mastery and integration of the component knowledge and skills in the conduct of the task to produce a desired result. These component knowledge and skills are competencies. Thus, an 80/20 rule applies here: 80% of the important actions for successful job performance are controlled by 20% of the competencies used in the job (Cavallaro, 1987).

People carry with them a wide assortment of knowledge, abilities, interests, traits, and motives, and when these attributes relate demonstrably to doing a job well, they become job competencies (Klemp, Jr. 1982). To define competencies for a staff developer is to determine the particular interaction of skills, knowledge, attitudes, behaviors, motives, self-image, social role, traits, and/or intellectual strategies which lead to superior job performance.

Role/Task Competency

Regarded as important by both the superior performers and average performers are an individual's ability to perform tasks related to three major roles: the Learning Specialist, Administrator, and Consultant (Nadler, 1980). These three major roles and 11 subroles comprise the Nadler Human Resource Development (HRD) Practitioner Role/Activity Model, which is validated in over 100 studies. A literature review demonstrates that the role and tasks of the HRD Practitioner are parallel to those of the staff developer. Therefore, the Nadler Model is used as the foundation from which the tasks/activities and technical knowledge and skills of the staff developer are derived. The Nadler Model appears in Figure 11.1. While these roles inevitably overlap, they provide a useful division for examination. A brief description of each role in terms of its corresponding duties and responsibilities is described.

Learning Specialist

A learning specialist focuses primarily on the design, development, and delivery of either formal programs or informal, on-the-job learning experiences. Responsibilities typically include needs assessment, program design, materials and media development, and program delivery.

Figure 11.1
Activities and Roles of the Human Resource Developer

Learning Specialist

1. *Facilitator of Learning:* Works directly with the learner as an instructor, teacher, coach, counselor, or in conjunction with machine-mediated instruction.
2. *Curriculum Builder:* Designs learning experiences through appropriate uses of adult learning theory and frequently with subject matter specialists.
3. *Instructional Strategies Developer:* Develops the methods, techniques, materials, and devices to supplement the learning design.

Administrator

1. *Developer of HRD Personnel:* Provides for the continuing growth of HRD staff.
2. *Supervisor of HRD Programs:* Performs the usual supervisory functions for programs being developed as well as those being conducted.
3. *Maintainer of Relations:* Provides for continuous communication with various groups and individuals, both internal and external to the organization.
4. *Arranger of Facilities and Finances:* Prepares budgets and plans for facilities design and use.

Consultant

1. *Advocate:* Recommends appropriate actions to management regarding HRD.
2. *Expert:* Provides management with the range of choices from which they can make the necessary management decisions about HRD.
3. *Stimulator:* Encourages management with the range of choices from which they can make the necessary management decisions about HRD.
4. *Change Agent:* Assists management in identifying needed areas of change and provides assistance in planning for change.

Administrator

A staff development administrator manages educational staff and programs focusing on the acquisitions, allocation, and control of resources dedicated to the staff development function. Duties include recruiting, selecting, training, and evaluating staff development personnel; strategic planning for staff development; marketing staff development programs; budgeting; scheduling; and aligning the staff development function with the organization's (school district, building, consortium) strategic mission.

Consultant

The staff development consultant facilitates the change of individuals, groups, or organizations. Responsibilities typically include targeting a problem, collecting data on probable causes, proposing an intervention strategy, assisting with the implementation of the change program, and measuring the results of the change effort. Thus, this role has an emphasis on evaluation and research. To be an effective change agent, a staff developer

Without clear performance criteria, school districts select, administrators supervise, educators train, and purveyors consult to different (and sometimes even conflicting) images of the capabilities required to do the job.

should be prepared to add to the knowledge and practice of the staff development field. He/she is an intelligent consumer of research, including awareness of critical issues in staff development and the current research. He/she locates, assesses, and translates current wisdom into practical application. The staff developer is also able to determine the effectiveness of various staff development programs and to create realistic, yet scientifically defensible designs that demonstrate a program's impact.

Tables I-III in Figure 11.2 list those tasks of the staff developer necessary to superior, average, and minimum performance, respectively.

Technical Competency Within Roles

The technical competence component distinguishes differences existing between the superior and average performers. Most of the technical competencies which are similar for both superior and average performances occur in the tasks associated with the Consultant role. Most of the competencies which distinguish superior performers are associated with the Administrator role. In addition, superior performers value more highly those technical competencies relevant to the evaluation of workshops; e.g. the degree to which participants transfer learning and the degree to which a program has met individual- and district-level needs. These technical competencies are associated with the Learning Specialist role and are the only areas of that role ranked by superior performers as necessary for superior performance. The emphasis here is on research and evaluation and the development of knowledge and skills necessary to perform research and evaluation tasks effectively. Because of the importance attributed to these tasks a Researcher/Evaluator role could be added to the Learning Specialist, Administrator, and Consultant roles.

Figure 11.2
Tasks and Technical Competencies Necessary to the
Superior, Average, and Minimum Performance of
Staff Developers in Washington State

Table I: Tasks Necessary to Superior Performance

1. Prepares and circulates list of new staff development references and resources
2. Selects audio-visual equipment and materials
3. Reviews and selects proposals submitted by consultants
4. Coordinates preparation and delivery of materials and supplies to facilitators of staff development/inservice education activities
5. Arranges for set-up of facilities for staff development/inservice education activities
6. Maintains staff development resource library

Table II: Tasks Necessary to Average Performance

1. Selects learning strategy/methodology
2. Assists in continuing professional development of staff, including self
3. Develops guidelines for carrying out district's local staff development plan
4. Evaluates each workshop/inservice education session for participants' reaction
5. Assesses degree to which the staff development program has met its objectives in meeting the needs of individual staff and the goals and objectives of the district
6. Effects necessary changes in the district staff development plan
7. Prepares and disseminates announcements and descriptions of workshops/inservice education activities
8. Plans strategy for optimum staff use of workshops/inservice education activities
9. Negotiates with superintendent to determine scope of your input to define the training needs of educators in your district
10. Conducts the data gathering to assess staff development needs
11. Determines the staff development implications of proposed changes in mission, technology, and district organization
12. Guides district inservice advisory committee/task force and central office administration in the application of methods and techniques to facilitate the professional development process
13. Serves as central point of technical information of the staff development plan
14. Fosters "take charge" behavior in district in identifying and solving district staff development problems
15. Assists board of education, central office administration, principals, teachers, and support staff impacted by participants in staff development/inservice education activities in being aware of what a specific workshop/inservice education session can provide
16. Selects tasks to be subject of instruction
17. Writes goals
18. Selects methods to deliver training

19. Administers, collects, and processes the evaluation of the staff development plan using evaluation techniques and instruments
20. Determines annual personnel, facilities, and funding constraints for planning school inservice education schedules
21. Evaluates the products/services of consultants and provides direct feedback to the administration and consultants
22. Comments on and/or inputs into policies, procedures, and practices that affect the management process for staff development
23. Recruits future internal staff to function as workshop/inservice education session facilitators
24. Sets district's objectives relative to the planning of a staff development plan
25. Interacts with local training community
26. Selects, plans, and/or implements the training or other solutions of a performance analysis
27. Informs central office administration of staff development implications of proposed changes in mission, technology, and organizational structure
28. Evaluates each workshop/inservice education session for participant transfer of learning
29. Develops sequence of instruction
30. Meets all internal and external reporting requirements regarding staff development plan/program
31. Trains workshop/inservice education session facilitators in identified roles and tasks
32. Prepares cost reports of staff development plan and workshops/ inservice education activities
33. Communicates effectively your district's readiness to consult with others
34. Gathers information on OSPI long range plans, local staff development program goals, and district's mission
35. Prepares new or analyzes existing inservice activity plans with each inservice education session to insure they meet overall inservice education session objectives
36. Conducts instruction as outlined in lesson plans
37. Writes performance and knowledge objectives
38. Develops procedures for contracting resources: A/V aids, supplies, guest speakers, film production, etc.
39. Insures compliance with new state continuing education requirements and guidelines
40. Identifies and schedules use of facilities for staff development/inservice education sessions
41. Keeps records/monitors staff participation in staff development program
42. Specifies job performance requirements for each task selected to be the subject of instruction, including proficiency levels for tasks
43. Develops lesson objectives for each activity of the inservice education session

(Fig. 11.2, cont.)

44. Interprets and applies non-training regulations, policies, procedures, and practices that affect district operations
45. Maintains support system for staff

Table III: Tasks Necessary to Minimum Performance

1. Prepares specifications for requests for proposals

Table IV: Technical Competencies (Knowledge and Skill)
Contributing to Superior Performance

1. Skill in translating organization and participant needs into goal statements
2. Knowledge of the advantages and disadvantages of the following methods of instruction: Discussion Groups
3. Knowledge of the advantages and disadvantages of the following methods of instruction: Questioning Technique
4. Knowledge of the advantages and disadvantages of the following methods of instruction: Seminar
5. Knowledge of the advantages and disadvantages of the following methods of instruction: Peer Coaching
6. Knowledge of alternate means used to deliver training
7. Skill in selecting and developing support materials
8. Skill in serving as a subject resource person to participants
9. Knowledge of methods to compare on-the-job performance against established performance standards
10. Skill in administering criterion tests
11. Skill in using data for future planning
12. Skill in enabling participants to clarify directions for their own growth in accordance with their needs and those of the organization
13. Skill in designing the workflow and structure essential to the operation of the staff development plan/program within the organization
14. Skill in assigning and supervising the tasks of the staff development plan/program within the organization
15. Skill in establishing a system to identify potential instructors
16. Skill in communicating job roles and tasks
17. Knowledge of Washington State educator career and professional development opportunities
18. Skill in coordinating professional development programs with regional educational services
19. Skill in contracting with colleges/universities credit options for workshops/inservice education sessions
20. Knowledge of plans for the economic use of resources
21. Knowledge of methods to involve staff in the participation of a local staff development plan
22. Knowledge of methods to involve staff in the participation of a local staff development plan

23. Skill in managing district inservice advisory committee or task force agendas
24. Knowledge of theories of staff development management
25. Skill in using appropriate program evaluation techniques and instruments
26. Skill in using appropriate reporting procedures
27. Skill in determining criteria for measuring the knowledge and skills gained in training back on the job
28. Skill in using appropriate program evaluation techniques and instruments
29. Knowledge of implications of program evaluation results
30. Knowledge of method to develop plan for necessary revisions
31. Appreciation of advantages accruing from information and resource sharing
32. Knowledge of individuals and organizations in the local professional training community
33. Knowledge of institutions external to the district which impact staff development plan and programming
34. Knowledge of methods to predict staff development needs given the plans and goals of the district
35. Knowledge of specific training methods and techniques to meet desired training, education, and development objectives
36. In depth knowledge of staff development
37. Knowledge of how to define district's future setting
38. Knowledge of how to plan transition from district's present state to desired future state
39. Knowledge of how to move staff development to a desired future state while remaining compatible with needs of district and individuals
40. Skill in preparing educational parties to adapt change
41. Skill in facilitating change
42. Skill in negotiating, confronting, and resolving conflict
43. Knowledge of identified staff development/inservice education activities made necessary by proposed organizational changes
44. Knowledge of methods to establish and maintain communications to all educational parties concerning change

Table V: Technical Competencies (Knowledge and Skills) Contributing to Average Performance

1. Skill in analyzing existing training tasks
2. Knowledge of proper elements of performance requirement
3. Skill in identifying types of knowledge, skills, and proficiency levels for tasks
4. Skill in translating job performance measures into performance-based learning objectives
5. Knowledge of situations that provide participants with feedback
6. Knowledge of situations that prompt and guide the participants' practice of new knowledge and skills
7. Knowledge of practice situation to bring participant to criterion performance
8. Skill in grouping related blocks of instruction

(Fig. 11.2, cont.)

9. Knowledge of how the following types of learning influence course design: Cognitive
10. Knowledge of how the following types of learning influence course design: Affective
11. Knowledge of how the following types of learning influence course design: Psychomotor
12. Knowledge of how the following types of learning influence course design: A/V Assisted Instruction
13. Knowledge of how the following types of learning influence course design: Hands-on Practice
14. Skill in applying learning theories in the workshop/inservice education session
15. Skill in providing supportive and constructive feedback to participants during class
16. Knowledge of workshop/inservice education session evaluation methods
17. Skill in determining criteria for measuring performance
18. Skill in using performance evaluation measurement techniques
19. Skill in interpreting evaluation results to participants, administration, and district inservice advisory committee/task force
20. Knowledge of goals and objectives for the staff development plan
21. Knowledge of district's staffing needs
22. Knowledge of what kinds of facilities are required for inservice education experiences
23. Skill in meeting state record-keeping requirements regarding staff participation in staff development program
24. Knowledge of requirements and specifications of inservice education experiences
25. Knowledge of techniques for measuring participant reaction to the workshop/inservice education session
26. Knowledge of techniques for measuring the knowledge and skills gained in training back on the job
27. Skill in extracting information from computer print-outs
28. Knowledge of promotion, publicity, public relations strategies
29. Knowledge of intended audience of specific staff development/inservice education experiences
30. Knowledge of methods used to measure actual job performance
31. Knowledge of cost/benefit analysis techniques
32. Skill in analyzing the cost effectiveness of the staff development plan/program
33. Knowledge of cost/benefit analysis
34. Knowledge of the decision-making processes to help district personnel to meet desired training, education, and development objectives
35. Knowledge of the value of the specific staff development/inservice education in meeting individual needs and district goals and objectives
36. Knowledge of effective methods to inform all education parties of the value of a staff development plan and its specific inservice education sessions

Table VI: Technical Competencies (Knowledge and Skills) Contributing to Minimum Performance

1. Knowledge of the types of information needed to conduct a job analysis
2. Knowledge of the sources of performance date of prospective participant
3. Knowledge of task analysis procedures and uses
4. Knowledge of the components of a goal statement
5. Knowledge of the components of a behavioral objective
6. Knowledge of the conditions and standards used in developing objectives
7. Skill in using data gathered to write statements of learner outcomes
8. Knowledge of the method to analyze task statements to determine subtasks required for task completion
9. Skill in translating subtasks into behavioral objectives
10. Knowledge of criterion referenced testing concept
11. Knowledge of test validity and test reliability
12. Knowledge of retention and transfer tests
13. Skill in translating objectives into test items
14. Skill in constructing written test items
15. Skill in constructing performance test items
16. Knowledge of methods for sequencing objectives
17. Knowledge of general procedures to assist learning
18. Knowledge of staff development models
19. Knowledge of current concepts of how adults learn
20. Knowledge of the advantages and disadvantages of the following methods of instruction: Lecture
21. Knowledge of the advantages and disadvantages of the following methods of instruction: Demonstration
22. Knowledge of the advantages and disadvantages of the following methods of instruction: Role Playing
23. Knowledge of the advantages and disadvantages of the following methods of instruction: Problem Solving Exercise
24. Knowledge of the advantages and disadvantages of the following methods of instruction: Programmed Instruction Exercises
25. Knowledge of methods most appropriate for types of courses
26. Knowledge of types of media and A/V equipment
27. Knowledge of factors affecting the use of A/V equipement and materials in different learning situations
28. Skill in developing A/V materials to support learning objectives
29. Skill in organizing lessons that follow from the sequence of learning objectives
30. Knowledge of subject matter to be covered in workshop/inservice education session
31. Knowledge of methods to keep track of participant progress
32. Skill in communicating learning objectives and course content to participants
33. Skill in effectively using training aids and A/V equipement
34. Skill in recognizing class behavior problems

(Fig. 11.2, cont.)

35. Knowledge of performance standards of participants
36. Knowledge of district referral process for participants with exceptional concerns
37. Knowledge of related community and/or state support activities for participants with personal/academic difficulties
38. Skill in recognizing participant problems
39. Skill in translating approved staff development/inservice education programs into the budget
40. Knowledge of needs priorities set by staff development plan
41. Knowledge of the Washington State and local district system for determining staffing, funding, and facility needs for particular planning factors
42. Skill in computational techniques for staffing and budget
43. Skill in translating approved staff development/inservice education programs into the budget
44. Knowledge of district's contracting needs
45. Knowledge of district's contracting purchase procedures
46. Knowledge of requirements and specifications of proposed purchases
47. Skill in rating consultant proposals against established district and Washington State criteria
48. Skill in using district contract award decision-making process
49. Knowledge of required standards for products/services stated in contracts
50. Skill in using performance measurement techniques
51. Knowledge of staff development/inservice education program management procedures in other settings
52. Knowledge of RCW 28A.71.200/210 and WAC Chapter 392-195-015 (2)
53. Knowledge of district training requirements and guidelines as well as the results of the needs identification process
54. Knowledge of district and building's mission, philosophy, goals, and objectives
55. Knowledge of appropriate district reporting requirements — orally and in writing
56. Knowledge of state and other external reporting requirements — orally and in writing
57. Knowledge of prescribed formats for reporting
58. Skill in establishing a system for collecting information needed for reporting requirements
59. Knowledge of training and development concepts
60. Knowledge of personal motivation theories
61. Knowledge of district transfer system
62. Knowledge of district Personnel Manual policies
63. Knowledge of both internal and external facilities available for staff development/inservice education activities
64. Knowledge of procedures for acquiring facilities for inservice

65. Knowledge of matching facility characteristics to type of inservice education activity
66. Knowledge of A/V equipment operation
67. Knowledge of location of materials and supplies used for the inservice education sessions
68. Knowledge of available furniture and accessories for staff development/ inservice education sessions
69. Knowledge of available housing for participants and workshop/inservice education session facilities
70. Knowledge of housing needs for participants and workshop/inservice education session facilitators
71. Knowledge of district policies concerning housing
72. Knowledge of standards
73. Knowledge of procedures and prerequisites to participate in the district staff development plan
74. Skill in district record-keeping methods of continuing education units for participants in the district staff development program
75. Knowledge of definitions, policies, and procedures in RCW 28A.71.200/210 and WAC Chapter 392-195-015 (2)
76. Knowledge of techniques for measuring the knowledge and skills gained in training back on the job
77. Knowledge of available technical expertise in this area
78. Knowledge of methods in interpreting evaluation results
79. Knowledge of overall objectives of the staff development program
80. Knowledge of available program evaluation techniques
81. Knowledge of available technical expertise in this area
82. Knowledge of methods in interpreting evaluation results
83. Skill in using appropriate reporting procedures
84. Knowledge of graphics and reproduction services
85. Knowledge of individuals needing isnervice information
86. Knowledge of definitions and instructions to compile and tabulate data
87. Skill in using state-of-the-art computational procedures
88. Knowledge of methods to compute cost of inservice
89. Knowledge of current staff development literature, workshops, courses, etc. for professional development
90. Knowledge of special needs of each district building and individuals
91. Knowledge of budgetary limits
92. Knowledge of marketing/communications strategies
93. Skill in selecting strategy to your district
94. Knowledge of consulting theories
95. In-depth knowledge of staff development subject matter
96. Knowledge of terminology used by district central office
97. Knowledge of terminology used by OSPI/SSDC

Fig. 11.2, cont.

98. Willingness to see the OSPI/SSDC in terms of the interrelationships between the organization, its environment, the groups and individuals comprising the organization

99. Skill in defining how your district impacts on OSPI/SSDC internal and external environment

100. Knowledge of conducting reliability/validity studies

101. Knowledge of information gathering techniques

102. Knowledge of methods used to determine and measure job performance requirements

103. Knowledge of training or other solutions

104. Knowledge of the process of change

Figure 11.3
Staff Development Program Knowledge
and Skill Components by Role

Role	Knowledge	Skill
Learning Specialist	Curriculum interventions	Design a curriculum intervention
	Administrator development programs	Design an administrator development program
	Training styles Learning styles	Deliver a training session
	Instructional strategies	Design/use strategies
	Competency-based education	Develop a competency-program
	Needs analysis	Conduct a need analysis
Administrator	Strategic planning	Create a strategic plan
	Marketing	Create a marketing plan
	Education industry analysis	Analyze the education industry
	Forecasting	Use forecasting techniques
	Negotiation	Negotiate for program, space, equipment, money

Role	Knowledge	Skill
Administrator (cont.)	Staff development personnel planning; employee development	Development a plan for the recruitment, selection and training of staff to conduct staff development programs
	Facilities	Design a learning facility
	Culture	Analyze the culture of a school district/building
	Leadership theories	Create a leadership plan
Consultant	Organization development	Design an OD plan for use in a district
	Techno-structural intervention	Design a T-S intervention
	Process interventions	Design a process intervention
	Systems interventions	Design a systems intervention
	Team building	Design a team-building strategy
	Creative problem solving	Design a problem-solving program and a creative thinking program
Evaluator	Problem identification	Identify staff development issues
	Research literature	Review extant knowledge
	Program evaluation process; Experimental designs	Plan a program evaluation
	Tests and measurements	Create an instrument
	Data gathering techniques	Collect data
	Statistical analysis	Analyze quantitative data
	Qualitative data analysis	Analyze qualitative data
	Evaluation presentations/report	Submit results

Tables IV-VI in Figure 11.2 list those technical competencies (knowledge and skills) necessary to superior, average, and minimum performance respectively.

Looking at these staff development roles and the technical competencies within these roles an education training program for knowledge and skill components for staff developers is presented in Figure 11.3. This depicts Nadler's (1980) three roles as well as includes the Evaluator role. The knowledge and skill components are the recommended content for a preservice or inservice training program for staff developers.

Process Competency

Figure 11.4 displays the Behavioral Codebook. This codebook results from the content analysis of interviews of practicing staff developers in Washington State. These behaviorally-grounded themes with their corresponding behavioral indicators differentiate superior and average performing staff developers. This focus on the incumbents while they are engaged in their role-specific work (i.e., organizational performance) yields the process competencies. Those competencies which characterize superior performance are proactive leadership, strategic empowerment, collegiality, systematic implementation of strategy, and voracious learner.

Performance characteristics are competencies when they exist in a role in an organizational setting and are performed to an established standard.

Proactive Leadership

Superior performers display proactive leadership that shifted paradigms. They find new ways to change their organizations by integrating the old traditions, current realities, and future visions. Their vision stirs the consciousness of others and induces their commitment to sharing it as their own purpose and goal. They knew they can make a difference in establishing the school as an organization that promotes personal growth and improvement — for both students and educators. Their long range focus of an intuitive perspective causes them to look at the meaning of education and to emphasize creating a love for learning for all involved parties in the educational system. Therefore, they commit long hours and unrelentless energy to their vision which is carefully conceived, thoughtfully managed, and doggedly sustained. They do make a difference as they positively impact both student achievement and the personal and professional growth of educators.

On the other hand, the average performers verbalize the need to see the big picture and to have vision. Although they believe themselves to be persons of vision, it is, for the most part, the vision of another party which they articulate and align support. They themselves lack the ability to formulate a vision and articulate it to others. Furthermore, they are not integrators in that each staff development program appears to stand by itself and is not tied into the whole of the organization. They voice shared decision-making and horizontal relationships, but they dare not commit too heavily to them. In other words, although they feel they are significant in the change process within their organizations, enjoy their jobs, and exert great energy, the lack of purpose almost makes it seem like they are marching in time rather than making a difference. They adhere to the conventional bureaucratic paradigm as defined by Bertani and Tafel earlier.

Strategic Empowerment

In line with proactive leadership is strategic empowerment. Again, the average performers articulate the necessity to empower people and they believe they are doing so. However, they rarely give additional responsibility with authority. Although they hold a basic respect for the value of an individual and affirm the potential of people to change, they, at times, evidence the opposite. They are less willing to give others credit and are much concerned when doing so that their own credibility is enhanced in the process. Average performers look at others to primarily support themselves and their programs. Consequently, support systems are released too soon or they are retained, thereby restricting the independence of others. In other words, the average performer is more interested in controlling people than in developing people.

Superior performers are able to delegate jobs and decision-making to other people. They realize that this is the only way that others' actions and decisions count. They understand that management can not function otherwise. Not only are they sensitive and responsive to

Superior performers value more highly those technical competencies relevant to the evaluation of workshops; e.g. the degree to which participants transfer learning and the degree to which a program has met individual- and district-level needs.

provide structures for others' success, they celebrate the victories of others. Then, as others grow in independence, the superior staff developers remove the support and readily give them credit for their accomplishments. They always accentuate others' strengths because they acknowledge they are developers of others; they realize that the power of leadership enables people to be more successful to accomplish things that they think are important and to experience a greater sense of efficacy. In other words, the superior performer promotes the new "professional" paradigm which was also defined by Bertani and Tafel.

Collegiality

A collegial model characterizes the profile of the effective staff developer — a proactive leader engaged in strategic empowerment. Two of the behavioral indicators of this process competency are more strongly indicative of superior performers than average performers. These are "team building" and "matching individual needs to the group task." It can be concluded that superior performers are more skillful in creating a people structure, i.e. a collaborative culture. They construct such a culture within the context of personal growth and fulfillment. It is, therefore, a mechanism supportive of "leadership by empowerment."

Systematic Implementation of Strategy

No matter what the staff developer does, he/she follows a strategy for implementation.

Figure 11.4
Behavioral Codebook

Referent behavioral indicators are listed under their respective competency.

A. **Systematic Implementation of Strategy**
   1. Diagnoses needs
   2. Develops long range and short range goals
   3. Uses appropriate interventions, timing, and people
   4. Markets programs in multiple ways
   5. Evaluates in a formal manner
   6. Seeks evidence of transfer and impact

B. **Socialized Influence**
   1. Responds appropriately to organizational culture
   2. Effectively manages power issues
   3. Aligns collaborative support
   4. Forges links between organizational boundaries
   5. Negotiates win-win situations
   6. Packages ideas and sells staff development perspective to key decision makers
   7. Pursues overt and covert agendas
   8. Is available and accessible

C. **Sense of Efficacy**
   1. Is decisive (a "can do" attitude)
   2. States pride and accomplishments
   3. Recognizes strengths and weaknesses and works to improve*
   4. Is flexible (not afraid to adjust)
   5. Welcomes challenge and takes risks
   6. Demonstrates professional maturity
      (a) competent
      (b) confident
      (c) integrity
      (d) courage and convictions
      (e) copes with rejection
      (f) takes responsibility
   7. Self-energized

D. **Voracious Learner**
   1. Attends many workshops*
   2. Seeks models to improve student learning
   3. Reads professional literature
   4. Bridges theory with practice; ability to apply research
   5. Learns by and through teaching and doing

6. Models adult learning principles
7. Builds models

E. **Strategic Empowerment**
1. Respects the value of the individual
2. Gives credit to others
3. Enthused in seeing others grow
4. Delegates responsibility with authority
5. Is sensitive to others and responds with support for others' success
6. Holds others accountable to their best developmental interest
7. Builds independence in others

F. **Collegial Model**
1. Creates relationships between concerned parties where influence is mutually shared
2. Builds ownership
3. Uses group feedback for directives toward change
4. Forms teams from different levels of the organization*
5. Increases group participation by fitting needs of individuals to the nature of the task*
6. Respects multiple points of view
7. Builds trust and rapport among team members

G. **Proactive Leader**
1. Creates inspired vision
2. Articulates vision to others
3. Aligns collaborative support for vision
4. Bases vision on balance between logic and intuition
5. Desires to impact student achievement
6. Integrates ideas and activities into the institutional (educational) mission
7. One's behavior is congruent with his/her philosophy
8. Transforms conventional bureaucratic paradigm

H. **Maximizes Resources**
1. Uses cooperative efforts to share costs and resources
2. Demonstrates multiple use of equipment/resources
3. Establishes incentives to encourage professional growth
4. Networks with external environment
5. Collects information on resources
6. Sets priorities
7. Selects the best talent and puts it to work

* Denotes that this behavioral indicator strongly distinguished between superior and average performers.

This is another performance characteristic which moderately distinguishes the superior performer from the average performer. This competency is identified as the systematic implementation of strategy, and it is the step-by-step procedure for implementing and maintaining a plan. It includes developing long and short range goals, marketing and evaluating the programs, and seeking evidence of transfer of learning and impact.

Voracious Learner

Continuous learning is highly valued in that it enables one to improve his/her performance as a staff developer. Superior staff developers are more engaged in critical self-assessment than are their average counterparts. Perhaps, that is why attendance at workshops, conferences, lectures, and university classes is so much more a priority of the superior performer than the average performer. In fact, attendance at workshops is one of the stronger characteristics which distinguishes superior from average performers.

Implications for Training

These process competencies that most clearly differentiated the superior performer from the average performer differ in the way they can be taught and developed. A specific such as "forming teams from all levels," might be readily learned and incorporated into a staff developer's repertoire, while others, like "professional maturity," require a more basic and pervasive personal orientation and approach to the tasks. In this competency model of the staff developer, most of the process competencies fall into the latter category. This suggests some limitations on the ability to develop particular individuals for the role of staff developer solely through formalized courses or workshop-type programs. However, the increasing use of certain designs for learning such as discussed by Levine and Broude — mentoring and coaching — have real promise for substantive development of many of the process competencies. Proactive leadership, strategic empowerment, collegiality, and voracious learner are attributes which are more likely to be acquired through long-term association with and feedback from experienced, superior staff developers.

Conclusion

Previously, there has not been a clear definition of the tasks, technical competencies, and process competencies of the staff developer, and development of areas critical to the effective performance of the staff developer may have been neglected. This should not be the case any longer. The challenge for schools of education, state departments of education, professional educational associations committed to staff development, and purveyors of training programs and materials for practicing staff developers is to design learning programs based on these characteristics or dimensions of superior performance that really make the difference in the practice of staff development.

References

Cavallaro, S. (1987, March). *Design of management HRD programs: A competency model approach.* Lecture presented at the Corporate Learning Institute, George Peabody College for Teachers, Vanderbilt University, Nashville, TN.

Cavallaro, S. (1984). *A study to determine a method of identifying human resource development competencies at Coast Guard resident training centers as applied to the school chief role* (Unpublished doctoral dissertation, George Washington University).

Klemp, G.O. Jr. (1982). *Job competence assessment: Defining the attributes of the top performer*. In *The pig in the python and other tales* (collection of research papers presented before 1981 ASTD National Conference.) ASTD Research Series, Vol. 8.

Nadler, (1980). A model for professional development. *Training and Development Journal, 34(5)*, 14-22.

Solo, L. (1985). School site staff development: Structures and processes. *Education and Urban Society, 17*(3), 332-340.

Superior performers find new ways to change their organizations by integrating the old traditions, current realities, and future visions.

Superior staff developers are more engaged in critical self-assessment.

ANNOTATED BIBLIOGRAPHY

CHAPTER 1: DISTRICT-LEVEL STAFF DEVELOPMENT

Combs, A.W. & Avila, D.L. (1985). *Helping relationships: Basic concepts for the helping professions* (3rd ed.). Boston: Allyn and Bacon.

This book describes how to apply the research that was done at the University of Florida related to the helping professions. It specifically addresses the concept that the main thing which separates good helpers from poor helpers is the belief system that they have about the clients with whom they are working.

Dale, L.E., (1982). What is staff development? *Educational Leadership, 40*(1), 31.

This is a half-page statement about the confusion that exists over terminology used to describe Staff Development. It is useful in discussion groups to clarify the terms participants use.

Fullan, M. (1982). *The meaning of educational change.* New York: Teachers College Press.

Although published in 1982, this book still stands as a contemporary view of the concept of educational change. It is replete with examples and specific descriptions taken from what is happening from schools. It also provides a conceptual framework on the topic. Page 14 has a table that is useful in analyzing the staff development role in the implementation of validated innovations.

Goodlad, J.I. (1983). *A place called school.* New York: McGraw-Hill.

This widely read book has been described as a watershed for school improvement research. The concept of effective schools can be accomplished through the role of staff training with the school being the unit of change.

Guskey, T.R. (1985). Staff development and teacher change. *Educational Leadership, 42*(7), 57-60.

This four-page article does an excellent job of summarizing how different outcome measures of staff development relate to one another, and it challenges the traditional sequencing of these outcomes with a more contemporary sequence. The sequence is: (a) teachers change their classroom practices, (b) there is a change in their students' learning outcomes, and (c) there is a change in the teacher's beliefs and attitude about the innovation being implemented.

Hord, S., Rutherford, W.L., Huling-Austin, L., & Hall, G.E. (1987). *Taking charge of change.* Alexandria, VA: Association for Supervision and Curriculum Development.

This easy to read paperback is replete with charts and tables that clarify a complex set of conceptual frameworks which have come out of a 12-year study on change using the Concerns-Based Adoption Model. This should be on the "must read" list for every staff developer.

Krupp, J.A. (1986). Using the power of the principalship to motivate experienced teachers. *The Journal of Staff Development, 7*(2), 100-111.

This five-page article does an excellent job of summarizing the adult developmental stages and applies that conceptual framework to how to work with career staff members who are at different levels in their development.

Loucks-Horsley, S., Harding, C.K., Arbuckle, M.A., Murray, L.B., Dubea, C., & Williams, M.R. (1987). *Continuing to learn: A guidebook for teacher development.* Andover, MA: The Regional Laboratory for Educational Improvement of the Northeast and Islands.

This guidebook, which has been distributed to all members of NSDC, summarizes work currently being done by staff development practitioners throughout the country. It includes useful conceptual frameworks and a complete bibliography of references and descriptions that allow readers to make adaptations to their local situation. This should be on the "must read" list of every staff developer.

Metzdorf, J.N. (1987). Institutionalizing staff development programs. *The Journal of Staff Development, 7*(1), 88-91.

This four-page article includes the author's interpretation of specific items which must be in place if a staff development program is "institutionalized" in the school system.

Miles, M.B. (1983, Nov.). Unraveling the mystery of institutionalization. *Educational Leadership, 41*(3), 14-19.

The article deals with specific help in developing processes in which educational innovations can become an ongoing routine part of an institution.

Sparks, G., & Schiff, S. (1986, May). The triangle model of staff development. *The Developer, 1,* 7.

A two-page article in the National Staff Development Council's newsletter which describes how a complex staff development program can be categorized into three major parts. This is based on an analysis of an actual large-district staff development program.

Vaughan, J. (1983). Using research on teaching schools and change to help staff development make a difference. *The Journal of Staff Development, 4*(1), 6-24.

This is a 20-page synthesis of research on teaching and effective schools as it relates to staff development. It includes a four-page bibliography of studies and research findings that had been developed until its 1983 publication date. It still provides useful information for current staff development activities.

CHAPTER 2: ORGANIZING AND MANAGING SCHOOL-BASED STAFF DEVELOPMENT

Caldwell, S.D., & Wood, F.H. (1981, June). Inservice readiness: Do we have the cart before the horse? *The Developer,* 1-5.

An important component of inservice is the readiness stage, where one is concerned with obtaining teacher and administrator commitments to the goals for improvement that will be the focus for school-based staff development. This article describes the readiness stage and how it was implemented in the Ferguson-Florissant School District in St. Louis County, Missouri.

Joyce, B., & Showers, B. (1980, Feb.). Improving inservice training: The message of research. *Educational Leadership, 37,* 379-385.

This article reviews the research that clearly points out the need for coaching or follow-up assistance after inservice education. It is an excellent paper that identifies the kinds of support necessary to implement school-based staff development.

Lawrence, G. (1974). *Patterns of effective inservice education: Review of research.* Tallahassee, FL: Florida State Department of Education.

This is the most quoted review of research on staff development and one of the first comprehensive attempts to identify effective staff development practices.

Oja, S.N. (1980, Nov.). Adult development is implicit in staff development. *Journal of Staff Development, 1,* 7-56.

One of the important things to consider in designing inservice education programs is the nature of the adult learner. This article discusses important findings related to adult learners and implications for the design of staff development programs for teachers and administrators.

Sparks, G. (1983, Nov.). Synthesis of research on staff development for effective teaching. *Educational Leadership, 41*(3), 65-72.

A review of research on staff development programs that have focused on implementing effective teaching practices. The discussion is divided into three parts: (1) the content of staff development, (2) the process of designing staff development programs, and (3) the environmental factors that are essential for successful inservice programs.

Wood, F., Caldwell, S.D., & Thompson, S. (1986, Spring). Practical realities for school-based staff development. *Journal of Staff Development, 7,* 52-66.

This paper discusses the results of two case studies that were conducted in districts that were moving into school-based staff development. The focus of the research was on identifying the kinds of changes that would be necessary within the district and in organizing staff development for the district to accommodate school-by-school change. The authors point out that a move to site-based management changes the roles for principals, teachers, school board members, central office personnel, and the superintendent.

Wood, F., McQuarrie, F., & Thompson, S. (1982, Oct.). Practitioners and professors agree on effective staff development practices. *Educational Leadership, 43,* 28-31.

The results of research to validate the five stages of staff development (readiness, planning, training, implementation, and maintenance) are presented. A national sample of professors and practitioners who had expertise in staff development were surveyed. The study validated the RPTIM model described in the 1981 Association for Supervision and Curriculum Development Yearbook, Staff Development/Organizational Development.

Wood, F., Thompson, S., & Russell, F. (1981). Designing effective staff development programs. In *Staff Development/Organizational Development,* edited by B. Dillon-Peterson. Alexandria, VA: Association for Supervision and Curriculum Development.

This chapter describes a five-stage, school-based approach to planning and implementing staff development. An extensive research base is identified to support school-based staff development, along with specific examples of how effective practice in each of the stages has been implemented in model staff development programs.

CHAPTER 3: STAFF DEVELOPMENT AND THE INDIVIDUAL

Keirsey, D., & Bates, M. (1984). *Please understand me: Character and temperament types.* Del Mar, CA: Prometheus Nemesis Book Company.

This overview of learning style is technical yet practical. It proves particularly helpful for the individual who has limited knowledge of learning styles.

Knowles, M. (1980). *The modern practice of adult education: From pedagogy to andragogy.* Chicago: Association/Follett Press.

Knowles presents basic theory about adult learning. This book summarizes his seminal research and applies it to adults in learning situations. Must reading for those with limited knowledge about adult learners.

Krupp, J.A. (1981). *Adult development: Implications for staff development.* Manchester, CT: Project RISE.

An overview of the entire lifespan, giving the chief characteristics and developmental tasks of each age and stage and concretely applying them to staff development.

Krupp, J.A. (1982). *The adult learner: A unique entity.* Manchester, CT: Adult Development and Learning.

Thirty-four characteristics of adults to consider when working with adults. The book provides research support for each characteristic and concrete ways of applying the ideas to adults in learning situations.

Levinson, D.J., Darrow, C., Klein, E., Levinson, M., & McKee, B. (1978). *The seasons of a man's life.* New York: Alfred A. Knopf.

A research report on male development through age 50. Although a study of only 40 men, the book describes seminal research in the field.

McGuigan, D.G. (Ed.). (1980). *Women's lives: New theory, research and policy.* Ann Habor, MI: University of Michigan Center for Continuing Education of Women.

Research reports on subjects as diverse as black working women, working women with children, women and health, and women and life satisfaction.

Uris, A., & Tarrant, J.J. (1983). *Career stages: Surmounting the crises of working life.* New York: Seaview/Putnam.

Career issues that arise for individuals at different ages. Although somewhat general, it provides insights not found elsewhere.

CHAPTER 4: PUTTING IT ALL TOGETHER: AN INTEGRATED STAFF DEVELOPMENT PROGRAM

Most staff development literature focuses on school improvement, curriculum improvement, or individual professional growth. Guidance for district level staff development coordinators can be found in the following sources, as well as from articles and book chapters on organizational development. These sources do not directly address the question of how to create and manage a successful, integrated staff development program, but they do give useful research-based information and direction to district-based staff developers.

Dillon-Peterson, B. (Ed.). (1981). *Staff Development/Organizational Development.* Alexandria, VA: Association for Supervision and Curriculum Development.

See particularly: Albert E. Roark and Wallace E. Davis, Jr., "Staff Development and Organization Development."

Griffin, G. (Ed.). (1983). *Staff Development: 82nd Yearbook of the National Society for the Study of Education.* Chicago, IL: University of Chicago Press.

See particularly: Philip C. Schlecty and Betty Lou Whitford, "The Organizational Context of School Systems and the Functions of Staff Development."

Goodlad, J. (Ed.). (1987). *The Ecology of School Renewal: 86th Yearbook of the National Society for the Study of Education.* Chicago, IL: University of Chicago Press. *See particularly: Richard C. Williams, Kenneth L. Moffett, and Bruce Newlin, "The District Role in School Renewal;" and Richard L. Andrews. "The School-Community Interface: Strategies of Community Involvement."*

CHAPTER 5: DESIGNS FOR LEARNING

A number of general references are listed first. Next, references are grouped in several topical areas: support groups, cooperative learning, partnerships, coaching, mentoring, teacher advisors, teacher centers, networks, and independent learning.

Hall, G., & Loucks, S. (1978). Teacher concerns as a basis for facilitating and personalizing staff development. *Teachers College Record, 80*(1), 36-53.
Describes a client-centered model of staff development that matches teacher needs with intervention. Presents assumptions about innovative adoption and research to support individually tailored professional development programs.

Little, J.W. (1982). Norms of collegiality and experimentation: Workplace conditions of school success. *American Educational Research Journal, 19*(3), 325-340.
Reports findings from a study of six urban schools, emphasizing the importance of open communication, sharing, and talking about practice, mutual observations, planning together as key norms for teachers, and administrators seeking continued school success.

Loucks-Horsley, S., Harding, C.K., Arbuckle, M.A., Murray, L.B., Dubea, C., & Williams, M.R. (1987). *Continuing to learn: A guidebook for teacher development.* Andover, MA: The Regional Laboratory for Education Improvement of the Northeast and Islands.
The authors provide an overview of effective staff development practices and discuss the numerous alternatives available including specific structures, procedures, programs, and research.

McCarthy, B. (1983). Improving staff development through CBAM and 4MAT. In *4MAT system in action,* McCarthy, B., & Loeffler, S., (eds.). Oak Brook, IL: EXCEL, Inc.
Deals with improving staff development, suggesting a combination of the Concerns-Based Adoption Model (CBAM: by Gene Hall and Susan Loucks) and the 4MAT system — a teaching method that takes account of the specialized quadrants of the brain and their relationship to learning styles.

Parkay, F. (1986). A school/university partnership that fosters inquiry-oriented staff development. *Phi Delta Kappan, 67*(2), 386-389.
Describes a school-university partnership, identifying key principles of effective staff development. Change is predicated on open, honest inquiry into the teaching/learning process, involves two-way communication, time, and the establishment of new relationships among teachers and students. Program-related activities enhancing teachers' sense of professionalism are identified.

Sparks, G.M. (1983, Nov.). Synthesis of research on staff development for effective teaching. *Educational Leadership, 41*(3), 65-72.
Reviews the process of staff development and how it affects teacher change and improvement. Based on the premise that staff development includes three strands: goals

and content, the training process, and the context. *The author suggests specific training activities for teachers.*

Wilsey, C., & Killian, J. (1982, Oct.). Making staff development programs work. *Educational Leadership, 40,* 5-8.

The authors explain that incorporating research on adult learning, effective instruction, and principles of clinical supervision will provide a framework for effective staff development and training. They discuss the importance of matching the type of supervision model with stage of adult development, and present an overview of directive, collaborative, and non-directive supervision styles.

Wood, F.H., & Thompson, S. (1980, Feb.). Guidelines for better staff development. *Educational Leadership, 37,* 374-378.

Identifies current problems in staff development programs, including negative attitudes toward inservice education, lack of participant involvement in planning and implementation, and unclear objectives. Building on an understanding of adult learning, the authors suggest the conditions under which staff development can be more effective, stressing the importance of experiential learning and informal settings where adult learners can interact.

Wood, F.H., & Neill, J.F. (1978). Experiential learning: An ultimate approach to staff development. *Texas Tech Journal of Education, 5*(2), 113-122.

Looks at both the traditional belief that adults learn best through assimilation, receiving, organizing, and applying information and an alternative view of experiential learning, beginning with the application and then moving toward a deeper understanding.

Wood, F.H., Thompson, S.R., & Russell, F. (1981). Designing effective staff development programs. In *Staff Development/Organization Development*, Dillon-Peterson, B., (Ed.). Alexandria, VA: Association for Supervision and Curriculum Development.

Presents a list of assumptions about effective staff development, an in-depth description of a five-stage process for creating an inservice training system, and examples of the process implemented in schools.

Support Groups

Daresh, J.C., & LaPlant, J.C. (1983). Inservice for school principals: A status report. *The Executive Review, 3*(7).

Discusses the advantages and disadvantages of five approaches to professional development for principals: credit-bearing courses at colleges and universities, institutes, competency-based training, the inservice academy, and networking. A sixth model, the Principals' In-Service Program, creates collegial support groups for principals and allows principals to be responsible for their own continuous learning.

Hawley, D. (1985). The quality circle concept. *Principal, 65*(2), 41-43.

Describes quality circles and outlines the steps that these small problem-solving groups go through to reach a point where members can make recommendations or decisions.

LaPlant, J.C. (1986). Collegial support for professional development and school improvement. *Theory Into Practice, 25*(3), 185-190.

Describes a model of support for principals with the potential of changing school leadership behaviors and restructuring the way schools are run.

Cooperative Learning

Brandt, R., ed. (1987, Nov.). Theme issue on collegial learning. *Educational Leadership*, 45.

The entire issue is devoted to collaboration among educators in schools. Articles address cooperative learning, teacher training, peer coaching, and support groups.

Johnson, D.W., & Johnson, R.T. (1986). Cooperation among teachers. In *Circles of learning: Cooperation in the classroom*. Johnson, R.T., & Holubec, E. (eds). Englewood Cliffs, NJ: Prentice-Hall, Inc.

Discusses the benefits of professional support groups among teachers while creating cooperative learning opportunities for students. Focuses on basic principles of mastering a new instructional technique, effective implementation, the purposes of professional support groups, and the necessary procedures for creating and maintaining a professional support system.

Johnson, D.W., & Johnson, R.T. (1980, June). The key to effective inservice: Building teacher-teacher collaboration. *The Developer*, 1-7.

Identifies the benefits of cooperative learning experiences for inservice training including high understanding, mastery and retention of materials, positive attitudes toward knowledge and skills, high levels of motivation, high sense of personal efficacy, and positive peer relationships. Procedures for structuring cooperative activities are summarized.

Partnerships

DeBevoise, W. (1986, Feb.). Collaboration: Some principles of bridgework. *Educational Leadership*, 43, 9-12.

Identifies principles of a successful collaborative relationship between a university and school system. Stresses the importance of school-university partnerships in developing successful teacher preparation programs.

Lieberman, A. (1986, Feb.). Collaborative work. *Educational Leadership*, 43, 4-8.

Discusses the realities and benefits of collaborative work. Citing examples of a state and local school district collaboration, a university-school collaboration, and a teacher-district office personnel collaboration, the author illustrates the power of collaborative work as a means of professional development.

Coaching

Brandt, R. (1987, Feb.). On teachers coaching teachers: A conversation with Bruce Joyce. *Educational Leadership*, 44, 12-17.

Discusses the need for continuous training, the importance of having an active instructional leader, and the need for practice over time. Practice, feedback, and observation must be central elements if teachers are to be successful at coaching.

Garmston, R. (1987, Feb.). How administrators support peer coaching. *Educational Leadership*, 44, 18-26.

Describes technical challenge, and collegial coaching. Discusses how administrators can develop and maintain coaching in their schools.

Joyce, B., & Showers, B. (1983). *Power in staff development through research on training*. Alexandria, VA: Association for Supervision and Curriculum Development.

Deals with the importance of developing a knowledge base for teaching. Addresses the integration of research and practice, the necessary school climate and support needed for effective staff development, and the issues of transferring knowledge into practice.

Joyce, B., & Showers, B. (1982, Oct.). The coaching of teaching. *Educational Leadership, 40,* 4-10.

Identifies five major functions of teaching: providing companionship, giving technical feedback, analyzing application, adapting to students, and support. Emphasis on skill development and the transfer of theory to practice is made through a comparison between teacher and athlete, and their respective beliefs about skill acquisition.

Showers, B. (1985, April). Teachers coaching teachers. *Educational Leadership, 42,* 43-48.

Discusses the nature of coaching--including the purpose, process, and outcomes. Also addresses the role of coaching in relation to supervision and evaluation.

Mentoring

Krupp, J.A. (1987). Mentoring: A means by which teachers become staff developers. *The Journal of Staff Development, 8*(1), 12-15.

Defines and describes the mentoring process as well as a concrete plan for establishing a mentor program as a means of staff development.

Stavert Roper, S., & Hoffman, D.E. (1986). Collegial support for professional improvement, the Stanford collegial evaluation program. *OSSC Bulletin, 29*(7). Eugene, OR: Oregon School study.

Describes an evaluation system that uses teaches as primary evaluators of peers.

Theis-Sprinthall, L. (1986, Nov.-Dec.). A collaborative approach for mentor training: A workshop model. *Journal of Teacher Education, 37*(6), 13-20.

Critiques a current teacher induction program and offers a model of school-based teacher preparation through mentoring. Mentors will be trained and a goal of inservice teacher education will be to promote adult growth to higher order levels of reflection and action.

Wagner, L.A. (1985, Nov.). Ambiguities and possibilities in California's mentor teacher program. *Educational Leadership, 43,* 23-29.

Presented as one component of school improvement efforts in California, the MENTOR Teacher Program serves as a staff development resource for teachers. The author describes program implementation and successful programs.

Teacher Advisors

Mai, R.P. (1978, Aug.). Advisors and staff development. *The Developer,* 1-4.

Describes the concept of teacher advisor and the strategies used to make it an effective staff development design. Discusses the relationship between teacher and advisor. Presents specific examples of staff development emanating from the Teacher Advisor Program.

Little, J.W., Galagaran, P., & O'Neal, R. (1984). *Professional development roles and relationships: Principles and skills of "advising".* San Francisco, CA: Far West Laboratory for Educational Research and Development.

Describes a joint venture between the Far West Laboratory and the Marin County Teacher Advisor Project, specifically examining roles of the advisor and the dynamics of "advising" based on classroom observation.

Teacher Centers

Daveney, K., & Thorn, L. (1975). *Exploring teachers' centers.* San Francisco, CA: Far West Laboratory for Educational Research and Development.

Defines the teacher center concept as an alternative form of continuing education for teachers. Explores the communications network existing among centers and provides descriptions of 22 teacher centers in the United States.

Edelfeldt, R.A. (1982). Critical issues in developing teacher centers. *Phi Delta Kappan, 63*(6), 390-393.

Based on the premise that teacher centers enable teachers to gain support and stimulation as well as take greater control over their own professional development, the author suggests key questions and issues around governance, funding, policy, and membership that professionals should address in developing and maintaining successful teacher centers.

Rogers, V. (1976, March). Why teachers centers in the U.S.? *Educational Leadership, 33*, 406-412.

Compares and contrasts the British and American approaches to educational change. Emphasizes the need for local initiative rather than systemwide or statewide control. The teacher as professional and key change agent is discussed as well as the need for new teacher education preservice and inservice education to help teachers develop their potential.

Rogers, V. (1976, March). Teachers centers in the U.S.: An idea whose time has come? *Educational Leadership, 33*, 403-405.

Raises the concern that teacher centers are product oriented rather than places conducive to professional growth and change. Discusses the issue of funding, partnerships between centers and universities, program content, and membership.

Networks

Corbett, D.H., & D'Amico, J.R. (1986, Sept.). No more heroes: Creating systems to support change. *Educational Leadership, 44*, 70-73.

Discusses obstacles to school improvement and change including lack of time for educators to talk, observe one another and experiment with new ideas, minimal opportunities for rewards and encouragement, and insignificant time for organizational change. Proposes an educational system conducive to the support needed to improve schools.

Independent Learning

Knowles, M.S. (1986). *Using learning contacts.* San Francisco, CA: Jossey-Bass Publishers.

Discusses assumptions about adult learners as a foundation for individualizing and structuring learning opportunities for adults.

CHAPTER 6: CONTINUOUS IMPROVEMENT: CONTEXT AND SUPPORT

Academy for Educational Development. (1985). *Teacher development in schools: A report to the Ford Foundation.* New York: Academy for Educational Development.

This report is rooted in the documents resulting from various teacher development projects supported by the Ford Foundations since the late 1950s. After reviewing these projects, all aiming at some type of school reform, the Academy took a long look at related research on other public and private funded projects and prepared this document, which speaks persuasively about the relationship of teacher development to school

improvement, what teachers must know and be able to do, phases of teacher development, and roles for mature and especially capable teachers.

Griffin, G.A., ed. (1983). *Staff development.* Chicago, IL: The National Society for the
Study of Education.

*The 82nd NSEE yearbook contains chapters written by key people in the field of staff
development. Griffin's introductory and concluding chapters give focus and direction
for staff developers in how to think about their work. The chapter on adult learning as it
relates to teachers contains important considerations for establishing ongoing
programs.*

Lieberman, A., & Miller, L. (1984). *Teachers, their world, and their work.* Alexandria,
VA: Association for Supervision and Curriculum Development.

*This very readable account of the real world of teaching conveys a view as might be seen
from inside the teacher looking out. The authors take a giant step toward articulating
teachers' work so that those who plan to work with teachers have some clues about how
to successfully enter into those lives.*

Lieberman, A., ed. (1986). *Rethinking school improvement: Research, craft, and concept.*
New York: Teachers College, Columbia University.

*Old ideas and new images are the themes in this collection of essays and reports from
major contributors to the knowledge about teacher development as it relates to school
improvement. This volume contains materials that should assist a staff developer in
clarifying the importance of ongoing teacher development for school improvement.*

Patterson, J., Purkey, S., & Parker, S. (1986). *Productive school systems for a nonrational
world.* Alexandria, VA: Association for Supervision and Curriculum Development.

*This book will assist a "supporter" role person in entering into and working within the
organization of the school. It is especially helpful for understanding school culture and
its effects on the individuals working there.*

Schon, D. (1987). Educating the reflective practitioner. New York: Basic Books.

*How does craft knowledge get developed and transmitted? Schon gets us started in
thinking about possible new models for teacher preservice and inservice education.*

CHAPTER 7: ASSESSING PROGRAM EFFECTS

House, E.R. (1978, March). Assumptions underlying evaluation models. *Educational
Researcher,* 4-12.

*House describes the basic assumptions for eight evaluation models: systems analysis,
behavioral objectives, decision-making, goal-free, art criticism, accreditation, adversary, trasaction. The proponents for the models are identified along with the primary
audiences, methodologies, and typical evaluation questions. The philosophical under-
pinnings for educational evaluation are discussed.*

Little, J.W. (1982). Making sure: Contributions and requirements of good evaluation.
Journal of Staff Development, 3(1), 25-47.

*Judith Little describes her experience using systems concepts to evaluate a staff
development program. She provides 10 criteria that should be used to evaluate a staff
development program. These criteria include: gains in participants' knowledge or
skills, increases in the frequency and rigor with which recommended practices are used,
and strengthened commitment to testing and continuing effective practices.*

Marshall, J.C., & Caldwell, S.D. (1982). Information management and evaluation in staff development: A case report. The *Journal of Staff Development*, *3(1)*, 84-101.
This article presents an example of a management information system used for handling staff development program information. The system was implemented on a large mainframe computer system, but easily could be adapted to microcomputer technology. In addition, example evaluation studies using systems goal-based methodologies are described.

Scriven, M. (1967). The methodology of evaluation. In R.W. Tyler, R.M. Gage, & M. Scriven. *Perspectives of curriculum evaluation*. AERA Monograph on Curriculum Evaluation. Chicago: Rand McNally & Company, pp. 39-83.
In this chapter, Scriven discusses some of the primary issues associated with curriculur evaluation. Included in the discussion are: formative and summative evaluation, professional versus amateur evaluation, evaluation versus process studies, "intrinsic" evaluation versus "pay-off" evaluation, comparative versus noncomparative evaluation, and values and costs.

Stake, R.E. (1967). The countenance of educational evaluation. *Teachers College Record*, *68*, 523-540.
Stake recommends a straight-forward evaluation procedure that allows for the causal linking of program outcomes to preconditions set for the program and implementation of the program.

Tyler, R.W. (1942). General statement on evaluation. *Journal of Educational Research*, *35*, 492-501.
Ralph Tyler presents the six purposes of evaluation, including the periodic check on program effectiveness, validate hypotheses upon which the institution is based, provide psychological security, and provide a sound basis for public relations. In addition, Tyler outlines the six basic assumptions underlying program evaluation and provides suggested steps for conducting an evaluation.

CHAPTER 8: MANAGING CHANGE: AN INTEGRAL PART OF STAFF DEVELOPMENT

Fullan, M. (1982). *The meaning of educational change*. Toronto: Ontario Institute for the Study of Education Press.
This book provides a synthesis of a large part of the available literature and research on the change process, focusing on the key factors that influence successful implementation.

Hord, S. M., Rutherford, W. L., Huling-Austin, L., & Hall, G.E. (1987). *Taking charge of change*. Alexandria, VA: Association for Supervision and Curriculum Development.
Written for practitioners, this book describes and illustrates the major concepts of the Concerns-Based Adoption Model (CBAM), a model of how individuals experience the change process. Complete with diagnostic tools and discussions of appropriate interventions for various phases of change.

Loucks-Horsley, S., & Hergert, L.F. (1985). *An action guide to school improvement*. Alexandria, VA: Association for Supervision and Curriculum Development.
Another guide for practitioners, this book draws from research on the change process to

describe seven steps for implementing a school improvement project. From initiation to institutionalization, the steps are relevant for new practices or processes at the school or classroom level.

CHAPTER 9: INQUIRY-ORIENTED STAFF DEVELOPMENT: USING RESEARCH AS A SOURCE OF TOOLS, NOT RULES

References are provided in several topical categories: classroom management; cooperative learning; instructional supervision, coaching, and mentoring; and educational leadership and organizational change.

Classroom Management

Charles, C.M. (1985). *Building Classroom Discipline: From Models to Practice*. New York: Longman.
Presents seven models of discipline — from Neoskinnerian, to Glasser, to Canter. Many good ideas on discipline are presented for consideration by the teacher.

Doyle, W. (1986). Classroom behavior and management. In M. Wittrock (Ed.), *Handbook of Research on Teaching* (3rd Ed.). New York: MacMillan.
A technical chapter that reports the research on classroom management in detail.

Duke, D. (1982). *Helping teachers manage classrooms*. Alexandria, VA: Association for Supervision and Curriculum Development.
Contains edited chapters by researchers on teaching — Evertson, Brophy, Gump, and others. The topics are effective techniques, getting help, and school contexts.

Evertson, C., et al. (1984). *Classroom management for elementary teachers*. New York: Prentice Hall.
This is the manual used in the experiments referred to above. It contains detailed descriptions of the research and the techniques used by more effective classroom managers. Checklists, self-questioning outlines, and narrative descriptions of classroom activities are especially useful for the beginning teacher. (The version for secondary teachers is by E. Emmer.)

Wolfgang, C., & Glickman, C. (1986). *Solving discipline problems: strategies for classroom teachers*. Boston: Allyn & Bacon.
This book provides a clear and thorough presentation of behavior analysis, values clarification, Dreikurs, Glasser, behavior modification, assertive discipline, and Dobson models. Emphasis is placed on teachers' selection of a model in relation to children's stage of development.

Cooperative Learning

Cohen, E. (1987). *Designing groupwork: Strategies for the heterogeneous classroom*. New York: Teachers College Press.
The author treats groupwork from a sociological perspective and gives practioners valuable ideas for creating efficient groups that result in harmonious, equality-oriented classrooms.

Gibbs, J. (1987). *Tribes: A process for social development and cooperative learning*. Santa Rosa, CA: Center Source Publications.
This source explains the theory and details instructions for building cooperative learning

groups. It contains 121 activities, instruments, and resources.

Glasser, W. (1986). *Control theory in the classroom.* New York: Harper & Row.
This book gives a theoretical and practical view of how cooperation can be used in the classroom to improve students' sense of control and effiency, especially at the secondary level.

Johnson, D., Johnson, R., Holubek, E., & Roy, P. (1984). *Circles of learning.* Alexandria: Association for Supervision and Curriculum Development.
This book is a useful introduction to cooperative learning. It gives the research findings, essential characteristics, and guidelines for administrators and teachers.

Johnson, R., & Johnson, D. (1975). *Learning together and alone.* Englewood Cliffs, NJ: Prentice Hall.
A how-to-do-it book that many teachers and staff developers will find useful for experimenting with cooperative learning.

Johnson, D., & Johnson, R. (1975). *Joining together.* Englewood Cliffs, NJ: Prentice Hall.
Has an especially thorough presentation of the theory and practice of cooperative learning. It also has instruments that can be used for teacher inquiry.

Slavin, R. (1980). Cooperative learning. *Review of Educational Research, 50,* 315-342.
This comprehensive review of research on cooperative learning gives ideas on how research is conducted — the variables, constructs, and methods. The results are impressive.

Slavin, R. (1986). *Student team learning: An overview and practical guide.* Washington DC: National Education Association.
This manual gives step-by-step instructions on how to use heterogeneous teams in cooperative learning. Jigsaw, Teams-Games-Tournaments, and other strategies are described.

Instructional Supervision, Coaching, & Mentoring

Acheson, K.A., & Gall, M.D. (1987). *Techniques in the clinical supervision of teachers: Preservice and inservice applications* (2nd ed.). New York: Longman.
Rationale and specific procedures for using clinical supervision as a means of teacher growth. The book is uniquely helpful in providing thorough explanations and examples of various instruments for gathering and analyzing data related to classroom teaching-learning.

Brandt, R.S. (Ed.). (1985, Nov.). Making teaching more rewarding, thematic issue. *Educational Leadership, 43*(3).
This collection of articles concerns recent research and practices regarding career ladder plans, teacher evaluation, mentor programs, and professional development.

Brandt, R.S, ed. (1987, Feb.). Staff development through coaching, thematic issue. *Educational Leadership, 44*(5).
This is a collection of articles discussing strategies for successful peer coaching; contrasts between staff developer knowledge and skills required in traditional and innovative professional development programs today; and ways in which technical, collegial, or challenge coaching can be carried out in relation to individual teacher needs. A point-counterpoint set of articles clarifying appropriate use of Hunter concepts is also featured.

Christensen, J., Burke, P., Fessler, R., & Hagstrom, D. (1983). *Stages of teachers' careers: Implications for professional development.* Washington, D.C.: ERIC Clearinghouse on Teacher Education.

This is a concise summary of the research literature on early-middle-late career stages of teachers and the implications for staff development program content and pedagogical approaches. It is a helpful introduction to this dimension of individual differences among teachers.

Glickman, C.D. (1981). *Developmental supervision: Alternative practices for helping yeachers improve instruction.* Alexandria, VA: Association for Supervision and Curriculum Development.

This is a major book by a principal authority on the need to apply recent research on teacher development and individual differences to supervision. The use of directive, collaborative, and non-directive supervisory models is discussed in relation to variations in teachers' levels of commitment and levels of abstract thinking. Helpful case studies and a "supervisory-beliefs" diagnostic instrument are also included.

McGreal, T.L. (1983). *Successful teacher evaluation.* Alexandria, VA: Association for Supervision and Curriculum Development.

Presents a thorough and easily understood discussion of teacher evaluation which appropriately links evaluation to instructional improvement and employment decisions. The author provides guidelines for assessing and re-designing an evaluation system that considers local conditions and the latest research on effective teaching-learning.

Saxl, E.R., Lieberman, A., & Miles, M.B. (1987). Help is at hand: New knowledge for teachers as staff developers. *Journal of Staff Development, 8*(1), 7-11.

The authors present their research findings concerning the specific knowledge, skills, and attitudes of former teachers successfully working as "professional assisters" in school improvement projects. An overview of their related training modules now being developed and how they could be used for self-assessment and goal-directed growth is provided.

Educational Leadership & Organizational Change

Brandt, R.S. (Ed.) (1982, Dec.). Toward more effective schools, thematic issue. *Educational Leadership, 40*(3).

This collection of articles features major experts, their research, and case study examples from school improvement projects in a variety of sites across the country. Appropriate cautions are expressed that this body of research provides a framework, not uniform prescriptions, for local practice.

Deal, T.E. (1985). The symbolism of effective schools. *The Elementary School Journal, 85*(5), 601-620.

One of few articles that discusses the culture and symbolic meanings shared by people in effective schools. Helpful connections are also drawn between recent research on effective business management and effective schools.

Glatthorn, A.A. (1987). *Curriculum renewal.* Alexandria, VA: Association for Supervision and Curriculum Development.

A uniquely concise, practical, and thorough presentation of curriculum assessment techniques and related development guidelines for use by school practitioners wanting to better match district goals with curriculum. It clarifies how to strengthen curriculum using the latest research in specific content areas, at various levels of schooling, and in skill areas as critical thinking.

Greenfield, W. (Ed.) (1987). *Instructional leadership: Concepts, issues and controversies.* Boston, MA: Allyn and Bacon, Longwook Division.

Twenty-one recognized authorities examine contrasting meanings of instructional leadership; specific related practices; the mediating role played by school culture as context for school improvement efforts; the tensions existing today between administrators and classroom teachers regarding instructional leadership; and the implications of current models of professional development, teacher evaluation and incentive systems.

Hord, S.M., Rutherford, W.L., Huling-Austin, L., & Hall, G.E. (1987). *Taking charge of change.* Alexandria, VA: Association for Supervision and Curriculum Development.

The most practical, well-written, and convenient presentation of the University of Texas Concerns-Based Adoption Model, including innovation configuration, stages of concern, levels of use, and innovation adoption components. A useful discussion of the different but complementary roles played by teachers and administrators in successful change efforts is provided. The book includes data collection instruments, data analysis examples, and a bibliography.

Joyce, B., & McKibbin, M. (1982). Teacher growth states and school environments. *Educational Leadership, 40*(2), 36-41.

A thought-provoking discussion of research conducted regarding the reciprocal relationship between a school's professional development climate and the degree of interest and energy which individuals possess for growth opportunities therein. The article emphasizes that educational improvement efforts must involve contextual analysis of climate and values, and it suggests strategic ways for doing so and planning change accordingly.

Lieberman, A. (Ed.) (1986). *Rethinking school improvement: Research, craft and concept.* New York: Teachers College Press, Columbia University.

Twenty authorities who have conducted and studied school improvement in large-scale and single-site projects during the past 25 years discuss the cultural, organizational, and political facets of school improvement. Particular emphasis is given to the genuine enhancement of the teacher's role in reform. Contains a helpful discussion by authors re-thinking their earlier views in light of recent research about the simultaneous artistic and scientific, linear and non-linear, aspects of school improvement efforts.

Lieberman, A., & Miller, L. (1984). *Teachers, their world and their work: Implications for school improvement.* Alexandria, VA: Association for Supervision and Curriculum Development.

Parallel to the 1986, Lieberman Rethinking School Improvement *volume, with helpful emphasis on the teacher side of the typical school workplace. Contains a discussion of the typical school workplace environment in which teachers must function today. Research regarding important variables to consider when developing realistic strategies for enhancing teachers' performance, decision making, and morale is discussed.*

Loucks-Horsley, S., & Hergert, L.F. (1985). *An action guide to school improvement.* Alexandria, VA: Association for Supervision and Curriculum Development.

The title provides an accurate summary of this book's presentation of the practical use of research concepts, questions, data collection techniques and findings about school-

improvement strategies contained in the University of Texas Concerns-Based Adoption Model. A helpful index of school-improvement resources is contained in the appendix. The book is unique in including "conversations" between the authors that accurately portray the complexity and lack of certainty in decision making within school improvement efforts.

McEvoy, B. (1987). Everyday acts: How principals influence development of their staffs. *Educational Leadership, 44*(5), 73-77.

This article presents findings from a five-year research study concerning how principals exercise leadership. Emphasis is placed on the subtle, quick, informal ways in which teacher growth, experimentation, and goal-directed efforts are encouraged and rewarded.

Wiles, J.W., & Bondi, J.W. (1986). *Making middle schools work.* Alexandria, VA: Association for Supervision and Curriculum Development.

This is a clear and detailed presentation of the rationale and various processes for assessing the current status of curriculum, personnel and facilities in a school with a related explanation of school improvement procedures. A strong integration of curricular, political and human components of school improvement efforts is presented which makes this book particularly useful even to those working at non-middle school levels.

ABOUT THE AUTHORS

Jan Austin is Assistant Superintendent for Curriculum and Instruction, Mill Valley School District, Mill Valley, California

Albert A. Bertani is Graduate Faculty Member, Department of Education Leadership, National College of Education, Evanston, Illinois

Nancy E. Broude is Program Coordinator, Principal's Center at Harvard University, Harvard Graduate School of Education, Cambridge, Massachusetts

Sarah DeJarnette Caldwell is Assistant Superintendent for Secondary Education, Webster Groves School District, Webster Groves, Missouri

Dian K. Castle is President, Educational Consultants I, and Manager of Professional Curriculum Development, Bell South Services, Atlanta, Georgia.

Susan S. Ellis is Coordinator of Staff Development, Greenwich Public Schools, Greenwich Connecticut

Barry A. Kaufman is Chairman, Department of Education, Dominican College, San Rafael, California

Karen Kent is Director of Expansion-Child Development Project, Developmental Studies Center, San Ramon, California

Judy-Arin Krupp is Consultant and President, Adult Development and Learning, Manchester, Connecticut

Sarah Levine is Associate Director and Lecturer on Education, Principals' Center, Harvard University, Cambridge, Massachusetts

Susan Loucks-Horsley is Program Director for Teacher Development, The Regional Laboratory for Educational Improvement of the Northeast and Islands, Andover, Massachusetts

Jon C. Marshall is Coordinator, West River Graduate Center, South Dakota State University, Brookings

Jim Metzdorf is Executive Director of Staff Development and Adult Continuing Education, Jefferson County Schools R-1, Golden, Colorado

Joanne M. Simmons is Associate Professor at Michigan State University, East Lansing

Georgia Mohlman Sparks is Assistant Professor, Eastern Michigan University, Ypsilanti

Linda Tafel is Graduate Faculty Member, National College of Education, Evanston, Illinois

Fred H. Wood is Dean, College of Education, University of Oklahoma, Norman